The Nez Percé Campaign, 1877

The assault on the Nez Percé village

The Nez Percé Campaign, 1877

Two Accounts of Chief Joseph and
the Defeat of the Nez Percé

The Battle of Big Hole

by G. O. Shields

•

Chief Joseph, the Nez Percé

by Edmond Stephen Meany

LEONAUR

*The Nez Percé Campaign, 1877: Two Accounts of Chief Joseph
and the Defeat of the Nez Percé
The Battle of Big Hole*
by G. O. Shields
with
Chief Joseph, the Nez Percé
by Edmond Stephen Meany

Published by Leonaur Ltd

Copyright in this form © 2010 Leonaur Ltd

ISBN: 978-0-85706-230-7 (hardcover)
ISBN: 978-0-85706-229-1 (softcover)

http://www.leonaur.com

Contents

The Battle of Big Hole

by G. O. Shields

Introduction

Camp Pilot Butte
Wyoming
March 17 1889
Mr. G. O. Shields
Chicago, Ill.
Dear Sir:
I have read with a great deal of interest and pleasure the manuscript of your book, entitled "The Battle of the Big Hole," and as a participant in the tragic affair it describes, can cheerfully commend it to all who are interested in obtaining a true history of the Nez Percé campaign. It is a graphic and truthful account of the Big Hole fight, and of the events leading up to it, and must prove a most valuable contribution to the history of our Indian wars.

I trust the book will meet with the generous reception it deserves.

Yours truly,
Chas. A. Coolidge
Captain
Seventh U.S. Infantry.

Chapter 1

The Nez Percé Indians are a powerful and populous tribe, who, for centuries, have made their home in the Snake, Salmon, and Clear Water Valleys in Washington, Oregon, and Idaho. When the great tide of civilization, which for years flowed toward the Pacific Coast, finally spread out into these valleys, questions arose between the emigrants and Indians as to the ownership of certain lands claimed by the latter, and the United States Government sought to settle these questions amicably. Commissioners were appointed and sent out to investigate and define the rights of the Indians, and in 1853, a treaty was concluded between the United States and the head chiefs and fifty-two of the principal men of the Nez Percé tribe, defining the boundaries of the country claimed by them, and ceding to the Government certain other lands which they had formerly occupied, but to which they had set up no valid claim.

In 1863, another treaty was made, modifying these boundaries to some extent, and in 1868, still another was negotiated at Washington that was finally signed by "Lawyer," head chief of the Nez Percés, and by "Timothy" and "Jason," sub-chiefs, all of whom claimed to be, and in fact were, acting for the entire tribe by virtue of authority given them by the tribal laws, and by a general council of their people assembled for that purpose.

In this treaty, the Indians agreed, for certain considerations that were entirely satisfactory to them, to relinquish certain portions of their reservation which they agreed were not needed or used by them, and to remove from said lands within one year from that date; to locate and live upon the reservation therein designated and described.

The tract relinquished to the United States in this instrument included the Wallowa Valley. When the chiefs returned to their people and reported their action, Young Joseph repudiated the treaty, and refused to be bound by it. He claimed the Wallowa Valley as the special home and inheritance of himself and his people, and said he would continue so to claim it, and to occupy it whenever he chose, against all other claimants, white or red.

In this dissension he was in time joined by White Bird, Looking Glass, To-hul-hul-sote and other sub-chiefs, and several hundred warriors. These became known henceforth as the "Non-treaty Nez Percés." Joseph and his band had never really occupied the valley permanently, and had never before made any special claim to it as against any other portion of the tribe. He had frequently gone into it during the summer to fish and hunt, in common with various other bands of the tribe, but had never staid more than a few weeks at a time, and had made his home during the greater portion of each year in the Imnaha Valley near the Snake River.

In 1871, a few whites settled in the Wallowa Valley. Joseph protested, became obstreperous, ordered them away, and threatened violence if they remained, but so far did nothing more than threaten. Other whites came in the following years and the complications increased. Com-

CHIEF JOSEPH

plaints were made to the Government that the Indians were annoying and threatening the settlers, and in 1875 President Grant issued an executive order, proclaiming that the Wallowa Valley was a part of the public domain and open to settlement by white people.

In May, 1877, Joseph and his band became more arrogant than ever, and again threatened immediate and violent measures against the settlers if they did not at once withdraw from his country. Some acts of violence were committed, and at the request of the settlers a company of United States cavalry was sent to the scene of the disturbance. The Indians were temporarily quieted, but the feeling of discontent and hatred against the whites was growing.

General Howard, then commanding the Department of the Columbia, repaired to the scene of the disturbance, and, with J. B. Monteith, agent of the Nez Percés, held several councils with the malcontents, and argued patiently and persistently to convince them that the treaty, whereby the Wallowa Valley had been ceded to the Government, was duly signed and ratified by the properly constituted chiefs of the tribe; that it was valid, and that every member of the tribe was bound by it; that the white men were only exercising their legal rights in settling on the land; and the Indians were assured that the whites would be protected in these rights by the white soldiers if necessary.

They were told in mild but positive terms that they must go on the reservation set apart for them by their chiefs and the agents of the white father at Washington; and warned that, in the event of their persistent refusal, soldiers would place them there by force, or so many of them as should survive in case they resisted. The three chiefs—Joseph, White Bird, and Looking Glass—finally agreed to go on the reservation, and asked for thirty days' time in which to collect their people and their horses and place them on the reservation. This was granted, and the council dispersed.

General Howard did not, however, place implicit faith in the promises of the wily chiefs. He suspected that this was merely a ruse of the Indians to gain more time for manufacturing sympathy among other members of the tribe, for gaining accessions to their own ranks, for procuring additional arms and ammunition, and, in short, for making all necessary preparations for active hostilities. He therefore proceeded at once to concentrate all available troops in his department within easy striking distance of the malcontents, in order to be prepared for any emergency.

Before the thirty days asked for had expired, some of White Bird's band appeared in the Wallowa Valley and murdered a number of defenceless white men and women. All the Indians in the neighbourhood became extremely belligerent and insolent. White Bird rode through the valley and proclaimed to the whites that the Indians would not go on the reservation; that they were on the war path and would kill all the whites, soldiers or citizens who should oppose their wishes.

As soon as news of this disturbance reached General Howard, he sent two companies of cavalry, under Captains Perry and Trimble, to the scene of hostilities, with orders to arrest the perpetrators of the outrages if possible, and bring them in. Captain Perry found the Indians in force in White Bird Canyon. They opened fire on him as soon as he came in sight, and he at once assaulted them. After sharp fighting for an hour, he was repulsed and compelled to retreat to Grangeville, a distance of sixteen miles. The Indians pursued him, and a running fight continued all the way.

He lost thirty-three enlisted men and one officer killed. Meantime, over twenty white men and women had been massacred at and near Mount Idaho, and a number of other women outraged in a most brutal and shocking manner.

General Howard then took the field in person, determined to punish the Indians who had committed these crimes, and to capture and place them on the reservation. Strong detachments of troops were sent in various directions, with orders to strike the hostile Indians wherever found. A number of sharp skirmishes and two severe fights occurred on and near the Clear Water River, resulting in severe losses to both whites and Indians. The troops moved so rapidly as to harass the Indians at every turn, and in several cases to intercept them when attempting to leave the country, and turn them back.

Finally, the main body of hostiles, numbering about 400 warriors and 150 women and children, by breaking up into several small bands, succeeded in evading the troops, concentrated their forces on Weyipe Creek, and started for the "buffalo country" in Montana, by way of what is known as the "Lo Lo trail." As soon as this fact became known to General Howard, he sent couriers to the nearest telegraph station with a message to General Gibbon, then commanding the district of Montana, with headquarters at Fort Shaw, stating the facts, and requesting him to send out troops to intercept the hostiles, if possible, while he should follow them with such force as could be spared for the purpose.

On receipt of this message, General Gibbon sent an order to Capt. C. C. Rawn, then in command at Fort Missoula, to watch for the fugitives, to head them off, hold them if possible, or turn them back. Rawn immediately dispatched a scouting party, consisting of Lieut. Francis

GEN. JOHN GIBBON

Woodbridge and three men, with orders to proceed up Lo Lo Canyon to the summit of the Rocky Mountain Range, ascertain, if possible, whether Joseph was really coming on that trail, and if so, to report the fact to him (Rawn), at the earliest possible moment. Rawn in the meantime prepared his little command for action. Woodbridge failed to return within the allotted time, and fearing he had been killed or captured, Lieut. C. A. Coolidge was ordered to take two men and scout in the same direction, search for him and for the Indians, and especially to examine a trail that branches off from the Lo Lo on top of the Rocky Mountain Divide, some sixty miles from Missoula, and ascertain whether the hostiles had gone that way.

These officers met on the divide, but no trace of the Indians could be found, and it was believed that they had either turned back or taken some other route. Both parties returned to their post, and reported the facts. Within a few hours after their arrival, however, two Indian runners came through, bearing messages from Joseph to the commanding officer at Missoula and to the citizens in the Bitter Root Valley, to the effect that Joseph and his band were coming over the Lo Lo trail; that they desired to pass through the Bitter Root Valley, *en route* to the "buffalo country," and assuring the people that if allowed to do so peaceably they would not harm the settlers or their property.

It subsequently transpired that Joseph and his band reached the summit of the range only three hours after Coolidge and Woodbridge had started on their return to the post. Joseph's messengers were promptly arrested, placed in the guard-house, and kept there until the end of the campaign. But the news they brought spread like wild fire, and the whole country was alarmed. Captain Rawn's command consisted of only two companies—his own and Capt. William Logan's (A and I), of the Seventh Infantry.

Leaving twenty men to guard the post, Captain Rawn moved at once with the remainder of his force, numbering about fifty men, up Lo Lo Creek. He was joined *en route* by about one hundred citizens from the town and surrounding country. At the mouth of the canyon he halted and built a temporary barricade by felling trees across it and up the north wall to a considerable distance, the south wall being deemed impregnable without fortifying. The slope to the right was gradual and cut up with gulches and ravines, some of which extended clear to the top of the mountain.

The next day after Rawn took up this position, Joseph and his followers arrived in front of the works, sent in a messenger with a flag of truce, asking again that he might be allowed to pass quietly into and through the valley. Rawn replied that the only condition upon which he would be allowed to pass, was that he and his warriors should surrender their arms. This the Indians of course refused to do, and a parley was begun that was prolonged through two days. Many of the citizens urged Rawn to allow the hostiles to pass on their own terms. They insisted that to fight Joseph there, with their handful of men, could only result in defeat, and that if he were compelled to fight at that point, and gained a victory, as he surely would, he would then leave a trail of blood and ashes behind him through the whole length of the valley. Others were more confident of success, and were spoiling for a fight then and there, but when, later on, a fight became imminent, several of these same citizens remembered that they had urgent business at home.

On the evening of the second day, the negotiations having failed, Joseph notified Rawn that he should go into the valley the next morning in spite of all opposition. Accordingly at daylight, firing was heard on the skirmish line, and it was supposed that the Indians would at once assault the main line. Stray shots continued for some time, and, as all the attention of officers and men was concentrated on the front, a man called attention of Lieutenant Coolidge to the fact that he had seen the heads of a few Indians moving down one of the gulches in the rear of the extreme right. This proved to be the rear guard of Joseph's outfit. The wily savage had outwitted the troops. He had left a few men to skirmish with Rawn's pickets, and while the command was expecting an assault in front he, with his motley band, had filed up and down through the gulches and woods, past the line of works, and was now well on his way down the creek. Rawn at once deployed his forces and pursued the fugitives, but did not overtake them until they had reached the Bitter Root Valley and turned up it.

Three miles above the mouth of the creek, he found them encamped on a ridge in a body of timber, where they had every advantage of position and cover. Their manner was insolent and defiant, for they seemed to consider themselves masters of the situation. Most of the citizens had now deserted Rawn; some because they believed the Indians had escaped and that there would be no fight, others because they believed Rawn would overtake them and that there would be a fight. Rawn's force was reduced to less than one hundred men, all told, and he saw that to attack the Indians in their chosen position, outnumbering him as they did, more than four to one, would be madness. He therefore wisely decided to return to his post and await the reinforcements that he knew were coming.

Some of the rear critics, who invariably talk loudest after the danger is over, who are "invincible in peace" and "invisible in war," have accused Captain Rawn of mismanagement, in allowing the Indians to pass him in the canyon, and of cowardice in not attacking them when he overtook them in the valley; but all who were there, and competent to judge, agree that the escape of the savages could not possibly have been prevented with the handful of men he had, and that he exercised judgment and discretion of a high order in not attacking them on their chosen ground, when such an attack could only have resulted in a repetition of the Custer massacre. His action proved, in the end, the wisest he could have taken in a strictly military sense; and, besides, it saved the Bitter Root country from being devastated; for White Bird said, afterward, that had the Indians been compelled to fight their way out of Lo Lo they would have fired the whole country, and many a ranchman would have lost his crops and his home if not his scalp.

But brave old General Gibbon, the hero of South Mountain, was on the war path. On receipt of General Howard's dispatch that the Nez Percés were coming his way, he hastily summoned Company F, of his regiment, from Fort Benton, and D from Camp Baker, to move with all possible speed to his post. Meantime he gave orders that Company K and every man that could be spared from Fort Shaw should prepare at once for the field. When Companies F and D arrived there, he took the field at their head, with the troops detailed from his own post, and moved rapidly toward Fort Missoula, crossing the Rocky Mountains through Cadotte's Pass, carrying a limited supply of provisions on pack-mules. The distance, 150 miles, over a rough mountainous country, was covered in seven days, the command reaching Fort Missoula on the afternoon of August 3.

On the 4th, with his command reinforced with Captain Rawn's company, and Company G of the Seventh from Fort Ellis, General Gibbon left Fort Missoula in pursuit of the Nez Percés. His command now numbered seventeen officers and 146 men. A wagon-train was taken from Missoula, wherein the men were allowed to ride wherever the roads were good.

The Indians had passed out of Lo Lo Canyon and started up the Bitter Root on July 28, and were therefore several days ahead of the troops. They knew that General Howard was yet many days' march behind them; that Rawn would not dare attack them with his little force of "walking soldiers," and not yet having learned the mysterious power of the telegraph wire to carry words, faster than the swiftest bird can fly, had not the remotest idea that another and larger force was on their trail.

They therefore moved slowly up this valley, resting and grazing their horses, trading off those that were worn and foot-sore for fresh ones, and buying from the ranchmen and merchants such other supplies as they needed, including *guns and ammunition*. Some of these avaricious whites not only sold the Indians all the supplies they could while passing, but actually loaded wagons with meat, vegetables, and such other marketable goods as they had, and followed up the dusky horde, selling them every penny's worth they could, as long as they remained in the valley.

The Nez Percés had for years been travelling through this valley on their annual trips to and from the buffalo country, on the Yellowstone and Missouri Rivers, and Chief Joseph and some of his followers had many personal acquaintances among the settlers.

Some of these whites openly boasted of their acquaintance and "influence" with the red handed murderers, and

1. Capt. Constant Williams; 2. Capt. C. C. Rawn;
3. Capt. William Logan; 4. Capt. J. M. J. Sanno;
5. Capt. G. L. Browning; 6. Capt. Richard Comba

gloated over the fact that it enabled them to sell them more goods than they could have done had they been strangers to the Indians. It is a well-known fact that there are a number of ranchmen and merchants in the Bitter Root country so greedy, so avaricious, so passionately fond of the mighty dollar, that they would not scruple to sell a weapon to an Indian, though they knew he would use it to kill a neighbour with, if only they could realize a large profit on it. In this case, they bartered openly with these cut-throats and assassins, receiving in payment for their goods gold that they knew was stained with the blood of innocent settlers, lately massacred on the Clear Water and Camas prairies, and from whom this gold had been pilfered. They provided the fugitives with fresh horses and other means of evading their pursuers, and so of escaping justice. A noble exception to this rule was exhibited, however, in the case of a Mr. Young of Corvallis, who courageously refused to receive their blood money, closed his store in their faces, and dared them to do their worst.

Of course, there are many good, fair-minded, honourable men in the Bitter Root Valley; but there are also a number of sharks, as I know by personal experience. There are men there who will charge a stranger, or even a neighbour, three or four prices for some commodity, and then if he ventures to protest against the extortion, will invariably answer him with that ancient bit of alleged humour, so familiar to the ears of travellers in the far West, to the effect that they are not out there for their health.

Joseph was reinforced in this valley by eighteen lodges of renegade Nez Percés, who lived off the reservation, under the leadership of the disreputable chief, "Poker Joe."

The hostiles did not keep their pledge with the ranchmen strictly. Near the head of the valley lived a man by the name of Lockwood, who, when he heard of the approach of the Indians, took his family to a place of safety. The Indians passed his ranch during his absence, broke into his house and rifled it of everything it contained that was of any value to them, including several hundred pounds of flour and bacon.

During the passage up the valley, White Bird is said to have scented danger, and to have counseled a more rapid movement toward the great plains. But Looking Glass replied: "We are in no hurry. The little bunch of soldiers at Missoula are not fools enough to attack us. We will take the world easy. We are not fighting with the ranchmen of this country." Poor, misguided savage! He deemed himself the wisest and most cunning of his kind; yet little did he know of the ways and resources of the white man.

Chapter 2

General Gibbon moved as rapidly as his means of transportation would permit, covering thirty to thirty-five miles per day. In his march through the valley he was joined by thirty-six citizens who did not sympathize with the kind treatment their neighbours had shown the fugitives, but who believed that they (the Indians) should be punished for their crimes, and who were anxious to aid the troops in administering the punishment. The pursuing party gathered all possible information *en route* as to the rate of speed at which the Indians were travelling, their numbers, etc., and from the citizens and the camp sites passed, learned that there were still over 400 of the warriors, and about 150 squaws and children in the band; that the bucks were all armed with modern breech-loading rifles, many of which were repeaters; that they were amply supplied with ammunition, and had with them over 2,000 head of good horses. Gibbon ascertained that he was covering two of their daily marches with one of his, and the question of overtaking them, became, therefore, merely one of time.

Near the head of the valley he fortunately secured the services of Joe Blodgett, an old-timer in this region, as guide and scout, who proved a valuable acquisition to his forces. The General had been previously assured that it would be impossible to take his wagons over the high divide between the Bitter Root and Big Hole Rivers, and had decided to leave them at the foot of the mountains and proceed with such supplies as he could take on pack mules; but Blodgett assured him that it would be possible to cross the range with lightly-loaded wagons, as he had recently taken such over himself. This proved valuable information, for the wagons and the supplies they contained were subsequently greatly needed by the troops.

When, however, the command reached the foot of the mountains and learned that the Indians had already crossed, a number of the citizens became discouraged and hesitated about going farther. Their affairs at home needed their attention. They were already out of provisions, and as it now seemed doubtful as to when or where the fugitives would be overtaken, they thought it best that they should return home. But the General knew that his handful of troops, veterans and brave men though they were, were scarcely equal to the 400 trained warriors in front of them, and appreciating the importance of keeping these hardy frontiersmen with him, he besought them to keep on a few days longer.

He assured them that he was in earnest, and should strike the Indians a terrible blow as soon as he could overtake them. He told the volunteers that they should have an honourable place in the fight, if one occurred; that they might have all the horses that could be captured, save enough to mount his command, and that meantime his men would divide their last ration with their citizen comrades. This announcement created great enthusiasm among soldiers and volunteers alike, and the latter at once decided to follow their gallant leader until the Indians should be overtaken, no matter where or when that might be.

Lieutenant Bradley, with eight men of the Second Cavalry, and all of the mounted volunteers, was now ordered to push on, strike the Indian camp before daylight the next morning, if possible, stampede the stock and run it off. If this could be done, and the Indians set on foot, then their overwhelming defeat would be certain. Lieut. J. W. Jacobs asked and obtained permission to go with Bradley and share in this hazardous undertaking. This detachment, amounting, all told, to sixty men, made a night march across the mountains, while the main command camped at the foot of the divide on the night of the 7th, and at 5 o'clock the next morning, resumed the march. The road up the mountain, a steep and difficult one at best, was seriously obstructed at this time by large quantities of down timber that had to be cut out or passed around, so that the ascent was very slow and trying to men and beasts. The wagons were but lightly loaded, and by doubling teams and using all the men at drag ropes, the command succeeded in reaching the summit, a distance of three miles, in six hours, and by the performance of such labour and hardship as only those can realize who have campaigned in a mountainous country.

From the summit the road leads down a gentle incline for a mile, when it reaches the head of Trail Creek, and follows down that stream a distance of ten miles into the Big Hole basin. It crosses the creek probably fifty times, and the banks being abrupt, and the road obstructed in many places by down timber, the progress of the command was extremely slow and tedious.

While ascending the mountain on the morning of the 8th, General Gibbon received a courier from Lieutenant Bradley, with a dispatch stating that, owing to the difficult nature of the trail and the distance to the Indian camp,

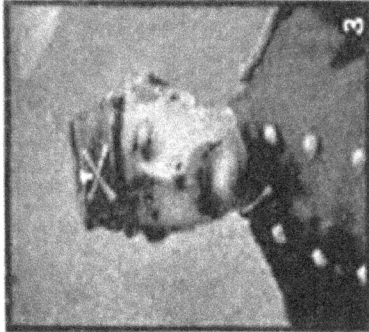

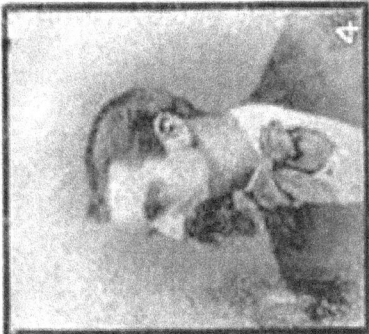

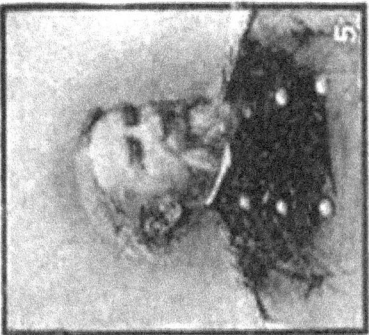

1. Lieut. J. H. Bradley; 2. Lieut. W. L. English; 3. Lieut. G. H. Wright; 4. Lieut. C. H. Coolidge

he had been unable to reach it before daylight, and that the Indians had broken camp and moved on. Later in the day, however, another courier brought news that they had again gone into camp, after making but a short march, at the mouth of Trail Creek, and that, not deeming it safe to attack in daylight, Bradley had concealed his command in the hills, and was now awaiting the arrival of the infantry.

Upon receipt of this information, Gibbon took his men from the wagons (leaving twenty men to guard the train), gave each man ninety rounds of ammunition and one day's rations, and pushed, on on foot, having ordered that the wagons should come up as fast as possible. The gallant General with his faithful little band moved quietly but rapidly forward, but owing to the bad condition of the trail, it was nearly sundown when they reached Bradley's camp. Bradley informed his chief that he believed the Indians intended to remain in their camp several days, for he had secretly observed their movements from the top of a neighbouring hill, and found that the squaws were engaged in cutting and peeling lodge-poles to take with them for use on the treeless plains of the buffalo country.

On arriving at Bradley's camp, the men filed into the gulch, ate a scanty supper of hard tack and raw pork, and, without camp-fires or blankets, laid down to rest. Having conferred with Lieutenant Bradley and his scouts as to the best disposition of the proposed attack, General Gibbon ordered his adjutant to call him at 10 o'clock at night, and lying down under the spreading branches of a pine tree, slept as peacefully as a child.

He knew there was bloody work at hand for him and his veterans; that the rising sun would see them contending against a savage foe that outnumbered his own command more than three to one; that ere nightfall many of

5. Lieut. A. H. Jackson; 6. Lieut. J. W. Jacobs; 7. Lieut. C. A. Woodruff; 8. Lieut. J. I. Van Orsdale; 9. Lieut. E. E. Hardin; 10. Lieut. F. Woodbridge

his noble men, and perchance he himself, would sleep their long sleep; yet he had a solemn duty to perform. It was a sad one; an awful one, but it was nevertheless a duty. He and his men were there to fight their country's battle. They were to avenge the blood of innocent men and women, whom these savages had wantonly murdered but a few days before in a neighbouring Territory. He had been ordered to strike and to punish them. He would strike, and the blow would be a telling one. Yet, in the face of these facts—facts that would chill the blood of any man unused to wars and scenes of carnage—this old warrior, this veteran of twenty bloody fields at the South, whereon he had behaved so gallantly as to receive merited promotion and congratulatory recognition from his superiors, was as cool, as self-collected, and could lie down and sleep as peacefully as though no enemy were within a thousand miles of him.

"Thrice is he armed who hath his quarrel just."

This old hero was to compete with a foe greatly his superior in point of numbers; a foe schooled in craftiness; a foe known and dreaded by every tribe of Indians in the Northwest; a foe who had stricken terror to the hearts of settlers and frontiersmen far and near; who had often camped on the ground he now occupied and knew every foot of it, while to the troops it was a veritable *terra incognita*.

Yet General Gibbon knew the men on whom he relied for victory. He knew they would stand by him, no matter what odds they might have to contend with. Thirteen of his seventeen officers were veterans of the war of the Rebellion, as were nearly all the citizen volunteers. The other four officers, and nearly all the enlisted men had seen years of hard service on the frontier, and had acquitted themselves nobly in many an Indian campaign. What marvel then that a man of such experience, and with such a record, in command of such men, and on such a mission, should feel an assurance of success that would bring sweet sleep to tired eyelids on the eve of battle?

Lieutenants Bradley and Jacobs did a piece of reconnoitring on this day for which they deserve great credit. Having failed to reach the Indian camp during the previous night, when it would have been safe to undertake to capture or stampede the pony herd; and knowing it would be rash to attempt it in daylight, it then became important to learn the exact situation of the village, in order that the commanding General might be given the most minute information concerning it when he came up.

Having secreted his command in the woods, therefore, Bradley sent out scouts in different directions with instructions to proceed cautiously and stealthily about the valley and ascertain, if practicable, the actual whereabouts of the Indians.

In about two hours these men returned and reported numerous fresh signs of Indians in the immediate vicinity, while one of them, Corporal Drummond, he said had, standing in the timber some distance to the east, heard voices and other sounds that evidently came from a busy Indian camp near by, but, fearing he might give an alarm, he had not gone near enough to the camp to see it.

Lieutenant Jacobs asked Bradley to let him take Drummond, return to the spot and verify such important information. Bradley replied that they would both go, and, leaving Sergeant Wilson in charge of the camp, both officers started with Drummond on foot.

They proceeded with the greatest caution a distance of about a mile and a half, when the Corporal whispered to Lieutenant Bradley that they were near the place where he had heard the voices. They were surrounded by a thick growth of small pine trees, through which it was impossible to see to any distance. Moving slowly forward, they soon heard the sound of axes, and inferred that the squaws were cutting lodge-poles in the very body of woods they were then in.

Creeping along with bated breath; on the alert for every sound or sign; fearful lest they should make known their presence to the Indians, bring on a skirmish, and thus avert the purpose of the General, they scarcely dared breathe.

They finally caught the sound of voices and stopped. Here the officers held a whispered consultation which resulted in their crawling ahead to a larger tree that stood about eighty paces in front of them. Still they could see nothing of the camp, although the sounds came plainer, and all were impressed with the knowledge that they were treading on the very crest of a volcano, as it were. Jacobs suggested that they climb the tree, arguing that as it was taller than those about it, they might be able to see something interesting from its top.

To this Bradley readily assented, and leaving their rifles with the Corporal and cautioning him to keep a sharp lookout for any possible intruders, both officers climbed cautiously and stealthily into the topmost branches of the pine tree. When they had gained this position, they halted for a moment in a crouching posture, and then, cautiously straightening themselves up, found that they were well above the surrounding foliage, and were thrilled at seeing hundreds of Indian horses quietly grazing in a prairie almost beneath them, for the tree stood on top of a high hill. Several herders sat on their ponies in and about the herd, while others lounged lazily on the ground under

SERGT. MILDON H. WILSON

the shade of neighbouring trees. A few hundred yards beyond, they saw the Indian camp where hundreds of warriors were resting and chatting, while squaws were pitching tents, making beds, carrying in poles, and cooking the noonday meal.

A brief look was all these brave officers dared risk, for they feared detection, and hastily lowering themselves to the ground, they lost no time in regaining their own camp.

A brief dispatch was sent off to the General, the receipt of which by him has already been referred to, advising him of their discovery, and the remainder of the day was spent in impatient awaiting his arrival.

Chapter 3

At 10 o'clock at night the officer of the guard spoke to the General in a whisper, and he arose with the alacrity of a youth who goes forth to engage in the sports of a holiday. The men were called at once, and in whispered orders the line of march was speedily formed. All were instructed to preserve the most profound silence from that moment until the signal should be given to open fire on the enemy, and, under the guidance of Joe Blodgett and Lieutenant Bradley, the little band filed silently down the winding trail, threading its way, now through dark groves of pine or fir; now through jungles of underbrush; now over rocky points; frequently wading the cold mountain brook, waist deep, and tramping through oozy marshes of saw-grass; speaking only in whispers; their rifles loaded, eyes peering into the starlit night, and ears strained to catch the slightest sound that might indicate the hiding-place of any lurking foe who might perchance be on an outpost to announce to his followers the approach of danger.

Five miles were thus stealthily marched without giving an alarm. Then the valley in which the troops had been moving opened out into what is known as the Big Hole, that is, the valley of the Big Hole River. This is a beautiful prairie basin, fifteen miles wide, and sixty miles long, covered with rich bunch-grass and surrounded by high mountains. In the edge of this valley the soldiers saw the smouldering camp-fires of the enemy; heard the baying of his hungry dogs responding to the howls of prowling coyotes, and saw, by the flickering lights, the smoky lodges of the warriors. The men crept up to within a few hundred yards of the slumbering camp, when they again crossed the creek down which they had been marching, and ascended its eastern bluff. Here they encountered a large herd of ponies, some of whom neighed anxiously as the strange apparition filed past them, but luckily did not stampede.

General Gibbon suggested to Bostwick, his post guide, that he take four or five men and drive this herd back up the canyon, but Bostwick replied that there was probably a strong guard over the herd who were sleeping at the moment, somewhere near by, but who would be awakened by any attempt to drive the horses; that it would take several men to whip them, and that the fight would alarm the camp. The General was so impressed with the scout's reasoning that he at once countermanded the discretionary order. It subsequently transpired, however, that the Indians had felt so secure for the time being that they had not a herder or a camp-guard out, and had Gibbon known this at the time he could have captured this entire herd without firing a shot, and thus have placed his enemy in a most critical situation.

Down the side of this steep bluff, thickly overgrown with sage brush, mountain laurel, and jack pines; over rocks and through break-neck ravines and washouts, the soldiers and citizens picked their way with, all the skill and adroitness of trained hunters, until at last they reached a position overlooking the Indian camp, and within 150 yards of the nearest *teepees*. The camp was pitched on the south bank of the Wisdom or Big Hole River, which is formed by the confluence here of Trail and Ruby Creeks. It was in an open meadow, in a bend of the river, and was partially surrounded by dense thickets of willows. There were eighty-nine lodges pitched in the form of a V, with the angle up the stream, and below the camp 400 or 500 ponies grazed peacefully, tethered to stakes and willows. The Indians had evidently secured them there in order to be prepared, ready for any emergency. The command halted here, and laid down to await the coming of daylight, but not to sleep.

It was now 2 o'clock in the morning, and the men suffered with cold, for even the summer nights are cold in these mountains, and they had neither overcoats nor blankets, having left all these with the wagons. The smouldering camp-fires flickered fitfully in the pale starlight, and the smoky lodges of the savages presented a most fantastic picture, as the dying lights blazed with ever-changing weirdness upon them. Eagerly the soldiers watched the scene, and with bated breath thought of the awful tragedy that the rising sun would look upon in that now peaceful valley.

"They have no idea of our presence," said Bostwick, the half-breed scout. "After a while you will see some fires built up if we remain undiscovered."

Sure enough, in the course of an hour, squaws began to come forth from their lodges and replenish their waning fires.

As these blazed up they stood about them, jabbered, turned, and warmed themselves, yawned, and then one by one returned to their skin couches and betook themselves again to sleep. And again the soldiers and their citizen allies were left to meditate, and in whispers to commune with each other.

Their thoughts and words were serious, for they well knew that where now all was peace, war in its veriest horror was soon to rage. The men doubted not that many of them would fill graves in that wild mountain valley before the morrow's sun should set, and that many others should suffer with grievous wounds. Yet they faltered not in their duty. On the contrary, they longed for the coming of the light that should enable them to see the redskins through the sights of their rifles, and complained only that it was too slow in coming.

Finally the night ended and the day approached from behind the eastern hills. As soon as it was light enough to see to move advantageously the little army was again astir; but its movements were yet as silent as the grave. Under whispered orders and with stealthy tread Sanno's and Comba's companies, deployed as skirmishers, descended the bluff into the valley, groped their way through the willow thickets, waded the icy river, the water coming nearly to their arm-pits. Logan, Williams, and Rawn, with their companies, were sent to the extreme right to cross and attack the camp near Ruby Creek, while Lieutenant Bradley, with his handful of soldiers and citizen scouts, was sent down the stream with orders to cross and strike the camp lower down. As the light increased the troops were advancing cautiously, when an Indian who had crawled out of his lodge and mounted a horse, rode out of the willows directly in front of Bradley's men and within a few feet of them. He was *en route* to the pony herd on the hillside above, and so quietly had the advance been made that even he had not heard or seen the men, and was within a few feet of them when he emerged from the thicket of willows. He and his horse were instantly shot down.

The order had been given, "When the first shot is fired

40

charge the camp with the whole line." And most eagerly was this order obeyed. Volleys were fired into the *teepees*, and with an eager yell the whole line swept wildly into the midst of the slumbering camp. The surprise was complete. The Indians rushed from their lodges panic-stricken by the suddenness and ferocity of the attack. They ran for the river banks and thickets. Squaws yelled, children screamed, dogs barked, horses neighed, snorted, and many of them broke their fetters and fled.

Even the warriors, usually so stoical, and who always like to appear incapable of fear or excitement, were, for the time being, wild and panic-stricken like the rest. Some of them fled from the tents at first without their guns and had to return later, under a galling fire, and get them. Some of those who had presence of mind enough left to seize their weapons were too badly frightened to use them at first and stampeded, like a flock of sheep, to the brush.

The soldiers, although the scene was an intensely exciting one, were cool, self-reliant, and shot to kill. Many an Indian was cut down at such short range that his flesh and clothing were burned by the powder from their rifles. Comba and Sanno first struck the camp at the apex of the V, and delivered a melting fire on the Indians as they poured from the *teepees*. For a few minutes no effective fire was returned, but soon the Indians recovered in a measure from their surprise and, getting into safe cover behind the river banks, and in some cases in even the very bed of the stream, opened fire on the soldiers, who were now in the open ground, with terrible effect.

The fire was especially destructive on the right or upper end of the line where the river made a short bend. As Logan, with a valor equal to that of his illustrious namesake, swept forward, he and his men found themselves directly at the backs of the Indians hidden in this bend, who now turned and cut them down with fearful rapidity. It was here that the greatest slaughter of that day took place. Logan himself fell, shot through the head, and at sight of their leader's corpse, his men were desperate. Regardless of their own safety, they rushed to the river bank and brained the savages in hand-to-hand encounters, both whites and Indians in some cases falling dead or wounded into the stream and being swept away by its current.

In twenty minutes from the time the first shot was fired, the troops had complete possession of the camp, and orders were given to destroy it. The torch was applied with a will, and some of the canvas lodges with the plunder in them destroyed, but the heavy dew had so dampened them that they burned slowly and the destruction was not as complete as the men wished to make it. Many of the lodges were made of skins, and these would not burn at all.

Though the Indians were driven from their camp they were not yet defeated. Joseph's voice, and that of his lieutenants, White Bird and Looking Glass, were heard above the din of battle, rallying their warriors and cheering them on to deeds of valour.

"Why are we retreating?" shouted White Bird. "Since the world was made, brave men have fought for their women and children. Shall we run into the mountains and let these white dogs kill our women and children before our eyes? It is better that we should be killed fighting. Now is our time to fight. These soldiers can not fight harder than the ones we defeated on Salmon River and White Bird Canyon. Fight! Shoot them down! We can shoot as well as any of these soldiers."

Looking Glass was at the other end of the camp. His

voice was heard calling out, "Wal–lit–ze! Tap–sis–il–pilp! Um–til–ilp–cown! This is a battle! These men are not asleep as those you murdered in Idaho. These soldiers mean battle. You tried to break my promise at Lo Lo. You wanted to fire at the fortified place. Now is the time to show your courage and fight. You can kill right and left. I would rather see you killed than the rest, for you commenced the war. It was you who murdered the settlers in Idaho. Now fight!"

Thus praised and railed at by turns, the men recovered their presence of mind and charged back into the camp. The fighting was now muzzle to breast. This deadly encounter lasted for some minutes more, when the Indians again took to the river bank and delivered their fire with great precision and deadliness on the troops in open ground. In the hottest of the fight, Tap–sis–il–pilp was killed. Wal–lit–ze, upon being told of his companion's death, rushed madly upon a group of soldiers and was shot dead in his tracks. Thus did two of the three murderers who were said to have brought on the war pay the penalty of their crimes with their own blood. The implied wish of their chief that they might be killed was realized.

Before these two men were killed, so says a surviving Nez Percé, an almost hand-to-hand fight occurred between an officer and an Indian.

The Indian was killed. His sister saw him fall, and springing to his side, wrenched the still smoking revolver from his hand, levelled it at the officer and shot him through the head. The Indian who described the event did not know who the officer was, but every soldier in the Seventh Infantry knows and mourns the squaw's victim as the gallant Captain Logan. Another Indian, named "Grizzly Bear Youth," relates a hand-to-hand fight with a citizen volunteer in these words:

43

"When I was following the soldiers through the brush, trying to kill as many of them as possible, a big, ugly ranchman turned around, swearing, and made for me. He was either out of cartridges or afraid to take time to load his needle gun, for he swung it over his head by the barrel and rushed at me to strike with the butt end. I did the same. We both struck at once and each received a blow on the head. The volunteer's gun put a brand on my forehead that will be seen as long as I live. My blow on his head made him fall on his back. I jumped on him and tried to hold him down. He was a powerful man. He turned me and got on top. He got his hand on my throat and commenced choking me.

"All turned dark and I was nearly gone. Just then a warrior came up. This was Red Owl's son, He ran up, put his gun to the volunteer's side and fired. The ball passed through the man and killed him. I had my arm around the waist of the man when the shot was fired, and the ball, after going through the volunteer, broke my arm."

Some of the Indians had, at the first alarm, mounted their horses, and rode rapidly to the hills on either side and to depressions in the open prairies of the valley. From these positions, as well as from the thickets and river banks, now came a most galling fire, which the soldiers were kept busy replying to. Although much of this shooting was at long range it was very deadly, and at almost every crack of their rifles a soldier, an officer, or a scout fell. General Gibbon, Lieutenant Woodruff, and both their horses were wounded by these sharpshooters.

Gibbon formed his troops in two lines back to back, and charged through the brush in opposite directions for the purpose of driving out the Indians who remained there, but they simply retreated farther into the jungle, ran by the flanks of the assaulting parties, and kept up their fire at short range. In this part of the action Lieutenant Coolidge was shot through both thighs. Lieutenant Hardin and Sergeant Rogan carried him into a sheltered spot near where the body of Captain Logan lay.

By this time Coolidge had recovered from the shock of his wound sufficiently to be able to walk, and, although weak from the loss of blood, picked up a rifle that had belonged to a fallen comrade and again took his place at the head of his company. While in this enfeebled condition he attempted to wade the river, but getting into water beyond his depth was compelled to throw away his rifle and swim. His failing strength now compelled him to seek shelter and lie down.

It soon became evident to General Gibbon that it would be unwise to hold his position on the river bottom, where there was no adequate cover for his men, and he reluctantly ordered them to fall back up the hill and take cover in the mouth of a gulch, since known as "Battle Gulch." They withdrew through the willow thickets to a position under the hill, gallantly carrying their wounded comrades with them, and then made a push for the timber. It was held by about twenty of the Indian sharpshooters, who were killed, or driven from it only at the muzzles of the soldiers' rifles. On the approach of the troops these Indians took shelter in a shallow washout, not more than a foot deep and two or three feet wide. Some of them were behind trees which stood beside this trench.

One had a few large rocks piled about the roots of his tree, and from a loophole through these he picked off man after man, himself secure from the many shots aimed at him at short range by the soldiers. Finally, however, a soldier, who was an expert marksman and cool as a veteran, took a careful aim and sent a bullet into this loophole which struck the rock on one side, glanced and entered the Indian's eye, passing out at the back of his head—a veritable carom shot. This tree was girdled with bullets, and the plucky Indian who lay behind it is said to have killed five of the soldiers before the fatal missile searched him out.

While the main body of troops were clearing out this clump of woods, the valiant band of regulars and volunteers who had been sent down the river under Lieutenant Bradley to strike the lower end of the camp, now turned and fought their way up through it; through the willow thickets; through the sloughs and bayous; through the windings of the river; killing an Indian and losing a man at every turn, and finally joined the command in the woods.

But the gallant young leader of the band was not there. He had fallen early in the fight; in fact, the first white man killed. He was leading the left wing of the army in its assault on the camp. General Gibbon had cautioned him to exercise great care going into the brush at that point, and told him to keep under cover of the brush and river bank as much as possible, but the brave young man knew no fear and bade his men follow him. One of them called to him just as he was entering a thicket where a party of Indians were believed to be lurking, and said:

"Hold on, Lieutenant; don't go in there; it's sure death." But he pressed on, regardless of his own safety, and just as he reached the edge of the brush an Indian raised up within a few feet of him and fired, killing him instantly.

The Indian was immediately riddled with bullets, and then the men charged madly into and through the brush, dealing death to every Indian who came in their way, and the blood of many a redskin crimsoned the sod, whose life counted against that of this gallant young officer. Thus he, who had led the night march over the mountains; who had by day, with his comrade, crawled up, located and reconnoitred the Indian camp, and sent the news of his discovery to his chief; who had on the following night aided that chief so signally in moving his command to the field and in planning the attack; who had gallantly led one wing of the little army in that fierce charge through the jungle and into the hostile camp, had laid down his noble life, and his comrades mourned him as a model officer, a good friend, a brave soldier.

Soon after the assault was made on the camp a squad of mounted warriors was sent to round up the large herd of horses, some 1,500 in number, on the hill-side, half a mile away, and drive them down the river, General Gibbon saw this movement and sent a small party of citizen scouts to turn the horses his way and drive the herders off. A sharp skirmish ensued between the two parties, in which several whites and Indians were wounded, but the Indians being mounted and the citizens on foot, the former succeeded in rounding up the herd and driving it down the river beyond the reach of Gibbon's men.

During the progress of the fight among the *teepees* the squaws and young boys seized the weapons of slain warriors, and from their hiding places in the brush fought with the desperation of fiends. Several instances are related by survivors of the fight, in which the she devils met soldiers or scouts face to face, and thrusting their rifles almost into the faces of the white men fired point blank at them. Several of our men are known to have been killed by the squaws, and several of the latter were shot down in retaliation by the enraged soldiers or citizens.

A scout who was with Bradley states that, while they were fighting their way up through the willows, he passed

47

three squaws who were hidden in a clump of brush. Knowing their blood-thirsty nature, and that several of his comrades had already been killed by this class of enemies, he was tempted to kill them, but as they seemed to be unarmed and made no show of resistance he spared them and passed on.

Two days later, however, while out with a burial party, he found these same three squaws all dead in their hiding-place. One of them now had a Henry rifle in her hands, and beside another lay a revolver with five empty shells in the cylinder. He thought they had recovered the weapons from slain bucks after he passed and, opening fire on some soldier or scout, had met the fate to which their conduct had justly subjected them.

All through that fierce struggle on the river bottom, officers fought shoulder to shoulder with their men; some of them with their own rifles, some with rifles recovered from killed or wounded comrades, and some with revolvers. Even General Gibbon himself—who, by the way, is an expert rifle shot—from his position on the bluff, devoted all his spare moments to using his hunting-rifle on the skulking redskins, and more than one of them is said to have fallen victims to his deadly aim.

Lieut. C. A. Woodruff, his adjutant, dealt shot after shot into the foe, as he rode from point to point, carrying the orders of his chief. Captains Comba, Williams, Browning, and Sanno, used their Springfields with telling effect and put many a bullet where it would do the most good. Lieutenant Jacobs was as swift as an eagle in search of his prey, and, with a revolver in each hand, dashed hither and thither hunting out the murderers from their hiding-places and shooting them down like dogs.

Lieutenants Jackson, Wright, English, Van Orsdale,

Harden, and Woodbridge were all at their posts, and none of them lost an opportunity to put in a telling shot. Lieut. Francis Woodbridge was the youngest officer in the command, then a mere boy, but a few months from West Point, yet he was as cool as any of the veterans, and displayed, soldierly qualities that endeared him to everyone who participated in that day's work.

Captain Rawn was at all times in the thickest of the fight, and was admired alike by officers and men for the alacrity with which he shared in every danger. His conduct in that fight gave the lie to the carpers who had accused him of cowardice in the affair in Lo Lo Canyon. In short, every officer, every enlisted man, and every citizen volunteer, fought as though the responsibility of the battle rested solely with him, and all acquitted themselves most nobly.

Chapter 4

As soon as the command abandoned the camp, the Indians reoccupied it, and under the fire of the sharpshooters, hauled down several of their *teepees*, hastily bundled together the greater portion of their plunder, packed a number of horses with it, and, mounting their riding ponies, the squaws and children beat a hasty retreat down the valley, driving the herd of loose horses with them. They had hot work breaking camp, and several of them and their horses were killed while thus engaged. Two of Joseph's wives and a daughter of Looking Glass were among the slain, who were believed to have been killed at this time.

When the command retired into the timber, the Indians followed and surrounded them, taking cover along the river banks below, and behind rocks and trees on the hill-sides above. The men dug rifle pits with their trowel bayonets and piled up rocks to protect themselves as best they could, and a sharpshooting fight was kept up from this position all day. At times, the Indians' fire was close and destructive, and here Lieutenant English received a mortal wound. Captain Williams was struck a second time, and a number of men killed and wounded.

Two large pine trees stand on the open hill-side some 400 yards from the mouth of the gulch. Behind one of these an Indian took cover early in the morning and staid there until late in the afternoon. He proved to be an excellent long-range shot, and harassed the troops sorely by his fire until a soldier who had crawled up the gulch some distance above the main body, and who was equally expert in the use of his rifle, got a cross-fire on him and finally drove him out. He went down the hill on a run and took refuge in the willows, but with one arm dangling at his side in a way that left no doubt in the minds of those who saw him that it was broken.

A large number of Indians crawled up as close to the troops as they dared, and the voices of the leaders could be heard urging their companions to push on. A half-breed in the camp, familiar with the Nez Percé tongue, heard White Bird encouraging his men and urging them to charge, assuring them that the white soldiers' ammunition was nearly gone. But he was unable to raise their courage to the desired point, and no assault was made. The troops held their ground nobly, wasting no ammunition, and yet returning the fire of the savages with coolness, accuracy, and regularity; and from the number of dead Indians and pools of blood found on the hill-side the next day, learned that their work here had not been in vain.

During the afternoon of the 8th the wagon-train and howitzer had been brought down to within five miles of the Indian camp, parked, and fortified by Hugh Kirkendall, the citizen wagon-master in charge, aided by the few men who had been left with him as train guard.

An amusing incident occurred that night, and yet one that came near costing Kirkendall his life. Among the men left with the train was William Woodcock, Lieutenant Jacobs' servant. He was armed with a double-barrelled shotgun and ordered to take his turn on guard.

During the still hours of the night the wagon-master was making the "rounds" to see if the men were on the alert. As he approached William's post the latter called out to him to "halt"; and, without waiting to learn whether his challenge had been heeded, blazed away at the intruder, whom he took to be a prowling redskin. The charge of buckshot tore up the ground and cut down the brush about the wagon-master, but fortunately none of them hit him. William showed himself to be a vigilant sentry, but a poor shot, and it is supposed that he will never hear the last of "Who goes there?—*bang!*" while there is a survivor of the expedition.

At daylight on the morning of the 9th three non-commissioned officers, and three men started to the front with the howitzer under the direction of Joe Blodgett, the scout. They succeeded in getting it up to within half a mile of the scene of action a little after sunrise. They took it across Trail Creek and up on the bluff, where they were in the act of putting it in position to open fire, when a body of about thirty mounted Indians saw it, and ascertaining that only a few men were with it charged with the intention of capturing it. Two of the soldiers who were with the piece became panic-stricken and fled when they saw the Indians coming, and did not stop until they reached the settlement a hundred miles away, where they spread the news that Gibbon's whole command had been captured and massacred. So far as is known, this is the only instance in which cowardice was shown by any man in the command.

The remaining four men stood bravely by the gun, however, loaded and fired it twice at the assaulting party, and then, as the Indians closed around it, used their rifles on them. When they saw that they could not successfully defend the piece, they threw it off the trunnion and retreated. Corporal Sayles was killed and Sergeants Daily and Fredericks wounded at their posts. The horses that were hauling the piece were both shot down. Private Bennett, the driver, was caught under one of them in its fall, and pretended to be dead until the Indians withdrew, when he took out his knife, cut the harness, and then prodding the animal, which was still alive, made it move sufficiently to release him, and he retreated and reached the wagon-train, where Sergeants Daily and Fredericks also arrived later in the day.

The Indians, finding the howitzer useless to themselves, took the wheels off the trunnion, hid them in the brush, and taking a pack-mule that had been brought up with the howitzer and which was loaded with 2,000 rifle cartridges, returned to their camp.

The loss of the cannon was a serious blow to the command, for, could it have been gotten into position and held, it could have done excellent service in shelling the Indians out of their strongholds, whence they so annoyed the troops. The piece could not consistently have been more strongly guarded, however, than it was, for every available man was needed in the assault on the camp. The loss of the 2,000 rounds of rifle cartridges also weakened the command seriously, for it compelled the men to reserve their fire all day, in order to make the supply taken into the action with them hold out. Had this extra supply reached them, they could have killed many more Indians during the day than they did.

Meantime the fight continued to rage at the mouth of the gulch, with varying fortunes and misfortunes on either side. Late in the afternoon a smoke was seen rising from beyond the brow of the hill below Gibbon's position, and the cry went forth that the Indians had fired the grass. A wind was blowing the fire directly toward the beleaguered band, and all were greatly alarmed. The General had feared that the Indians would resort to this measure, for he knew it to be a part of the Nez Percés' war tactics, and he believed that they intended to follow up the fire and assault his men while blinded by the smoke. Yet he was not dismayed. He urged his men to stand firm in the face of this new danger.

"If the worst comes, my men," said he, "if this fire reaches us, we will charge through it, meet the redskins in the open ground, and send them to a hotter place than they have prepared for us." The fire burned fiercely until within a few yards of the entrenchments, and the men were blinded and nearly suffocated by the smoke. But again the fortunes of war were with the beleaguered band, for just before the fire reached them the wind shifted squarely about, came down off the hills from the west, and the fire, blown back upon its own blackened embers, faltered, flickered, and died out. At this lucky turn in their fortunes the soldiers cheered wildly, and the Indians cursed savagely.

The men had left the wagons in the forenoon of the previous day with one day's rations, but in the charge across the river many of their haversacks had been filled with water, and the scant supply of food that remained in them destroyed. Others, more fortunate, had divided their few remaining crackers with their comrades who were thus deprived, so that all were now without provisions and suffering from hunger. The gulch in which they had taken cover was dry and rocky, and as the August sun poured his scorching rays upon the men they suffered for water. True, the river flowed within a few hundred yards of them, but the man who attempted to reach it did so at the risk of his life, and there were no more lives to spare. Not until nightfall did the commanding officer deem it prudent to send out a fatigue party for water. Then three men volunteered to go, and under cover of darkness, and of a firing party, they made the trip safely, filling and bringing in as many canteens as they could carry.

The men cut up Lieutenant Woodruff's horse (which the Indians had conveniently killed within the lines), and as they dared not make camp-fires, devoured full rations of him raw. The night was cold, and again the men suffered greatly for bedding. The Indians kept firing into the woods occasionally, even after dark, so that the soldiers were unable to rest. Once or twice they charged up almost to Gibbon's lines and delivered volleys on the men, but were speedily repulsed in each case by a fusillade from the entrenchments.

General Gibbon had heard nothing from his wagon-train since leaving it, and the fact that mounted parties of Indians were frequently seen passing in his rear made it extremely dangerous to attempt to pass to or from it. Indeed, he feared the train had been captured, for it was but lightly guarded, and during the night he started a runner to Deer Lodge for medical assistance and supplies. This man, W. H. Edwards by name, succeeded in making his way out through the Indian lines under cover of darkness, and walked or ran to Frenche's Gulch, a distance of nearly sixty miles, where he got a horse, and made the remaining forty miles during the following night, arriving at Deer Lodge on the morning of August 11.

On the morning of the 10th, a courier arrived from General Howard, informing Gibbon that he (Howard) was hurrying to his assistance with twenty cavalrymen and thirty Warm Spring Indians. On being questioned as to the supply-train, this courier reported that he had seen nothing of it, which statement greatly increased the fear of the men that it had been captured and destroyed. Later in the day, however, a messenger arrived from the train, bringing the cheering news that it was safe. The Indians had menaced it all day, but the guard in charge of it had fortified their position and fired upon the savages whenever they came in sight with such telling effect that the latter had made no determined attack. Howard's messenger had passed the train in the night without seeing it.

Early on the morning of the 10th, Sergeant Mildon H. Wilson, of Company K, with six men, was sent back to bring up the train, and later in the day, Captain Browning and Lieutenant Woodbridge, with twenty men, all of whom had volunteered for the service, were sent to take charge of it. They met the train on the way, in charge of Sergeant Wilson, and with it succeeded in reaching the command just at sundown, bringing the blankets and provisions so much needed by the men.

This detachment performed a hazardous and meritorious piece of work in thus rescuing and bringing up the train, for large parties of Indians were still scouting through the woods and hills watching for opportunities to cut off any small body of troops who might be found away from the main command and with whom they might successfully contend.

In the face of this danger, Browning and Woodbridge, with their few supporters, marched nearly ten miles through the swampy, brush-lined ravine, and succeeded in moving the train over roads that were well nigh impassable under the most favourable circumstances. The wagons had to be literally carried over some of the worst places, the mules having all they could do to get through without pulling a pound.

As soon as the train had been safely delivered to the command, General Gibbon asked for a volunteer messenger to go to Deer Lodge with additional dispatches, fearing that Edwards might have been killed or captured *en route*, and Sergeant Wilson, the hero of so many brave deeds, promptly volunteered for this perilous service. He started at once, rode all night, and reached his destination only a few hours behind Edwards.

The last party of Indians withdrew about 11 o'clock on the night of the 10th, giving the soldiers a parting shower of bullets, but it was not known until daylight on the morning of the 11th that all had really gone.

From the time the last shots were fired, as stated, all was quiet, and the men got a few hours of much-needed rest, such as it was, for they had slept but two hours in the past forty-eight. The fight was over; the enemy was gone. The sun that rose on the morning of the 11th, shone brightly over as beautiful a valley as the eye of man ever beheld, and the blackening corpses that lay strewn upon the field were the only remaining evidences of the bloody tragedy that had so lately been enacted there.

Acts of personal heroism in the fight were numerous, and it would be a pleasure to record them all, but at this late date it is impossible to obtain full particulars of this nature. Among those worthy of special mention, however, is this same Sergeant Wilson, of Company K, who, during the fight among the lodges, killed an Indian who was in the act of aiming at Lieutenant Jacobs, at very short range, and but for the quickness of Wilson's movements and the accuracy of his aim, Jacobs would undoubtedly have been killed. Wilson distinguished himself several times during the day, and is known to have killed several Indians. Indeed, it is said that his rifle seldom cracked but an Indian was seen to fall. He was subsequently promoted to regimental quartermaster sergeant, for gallant and meritorious conduct on that day.

Chapter 5

The Indians claimed after their final surrender that they would have held Gibbon's command in the timber longer than they did, and would have killed many more, if not all of them, had they not learned that Howard was at hand with reinforcements. They admit that they were warned of impending danger in some form in due time to have avoided a meeting with Gibbon, but did not heed it. They tell us that on the evening before the arrival of Gibbon's troops at the Indian camp, a "medicine man" had cautioned the chiefs that death was on their trail.

"What are we doing here?" he asked. "While I slept, my medicine told me to move on; that death was approaching us. Chiefs, I only tell you this for the good of our people. If you take my advice you can avoid death, and that advice is to speed through this country. If we do not there will be tears in our eyes."

But the chiefs heeded not his warning. They held a feast and a war-dance that night, and then lay down to sleep, feeling as safe as they ever did on their own reservation.

They claim to have received news of Howard's coming in this way:

When the troops retired to the mouth of the gulch on the morning of the 9th, the warriors were examining the dead. Among them they found a white man, a citizen, who was breathing; his eyes were closed and he pretended to be dead, but they saw that he was not though he was severely wounded. They took hold of him and raised him up. Finding that his "possoming" would not work, he sprang to his feet. Looking Glass was at hand and ordered the Indians not to kill him, reminding them that he was a citizen and that they might obtain valuable information from him. They then questioned him closely concerning the white soldiers. He told them that Howard would be there in a few hours, and that volunteers were coming from Virginia City to head the Indians off. While he was talking with them, a squaw who had lost her brother and some of her children in the fight, came up and slapped him in the face. He gave her a vigorous kick in return, and one of the warriors, enraged at this, killed him. The Indians having thus learned that reinforcements were close at hand, ordered the squaws to move camp, and the warriors remained to continue the fight, but in such light trim that they could retreat rapidly whenever it should become necessary.

The departure of the squaws had been so hurried by flying bullets that they left large quantities of buffalo robes, a considerable quantity of dried meat and other plunder on the field. They took all the pack-animals with them, however, so that the bucks were unable to take the property with them when they left, and it subsequently fell into the hands of the white men. One citizen volunteer gathered up thirty-two buffalo robes, which he subsequently took to Helena and sold at good prices as relics of the battle. Several of them were badly stained with blood, but this, of course, enhanced, rather than lessened, their value in the eyes of the class of buyers he sought.

Captain Comba was sent out on the morning of the

11th with a party of men to bury the dead soldiers and citizens, all of whom were found, recognized, and decently interred. Rude head boards, obtained by breaking up cracker boxes, were placed at the heads of the graves, on which were written, or carved, the name, company, and regiment of the soldier, or the name and residence of the citizen, whose grave each marked.

At 10 o'clock that morning General Howard arrived with his escort, and on the morning of the 12th, his medical officers reached the field and gave to the suffering wounded the first professional care they had had, for owing to the rapid movements of Gibbon's command, the surgeon who had been ordered to join it, failed to reach it. On the 13th, General Gibbon assigned to duty with General Howard to aid in the pursuit of the Nez Percés, Captain Browning and Lieutenants Wright and Van Orsdale with fifty men, all of whom volunteered for the service. Gibbon then left the battle-field with the wounded and the remainder of his command for Deer Lodge, where he arrived three days later. He was met *en route* by a number of wagons, ambulances, and nurses, sent out by the people of that town, and on arrival there, the wounded were carefully cared for, the command dispersed, and each company returned to its station.

Thus the Battle of the Big Hole had been fought and won and had passed into history. Thus more than a score of lives had been laid down and many men sorely wounded—some of them maimed for life—in another effort to teach hostile Indians the necessity of obedience to the mandates of their White Father.

Thus another page had been added to the glorious record of gallant deeds done; of bloody fights waged by our soldiers in wresting from the grasp of lawless savages the great and glorious West, and making it a land where industrious white men and their families might live in peace and safety. And every man, woman, and child who lives and prospers in that great West to-day owes the privilege of so doing to the brave men who for a quarter of a century have camped, tramped, and fought over the broad domain where now all is peace.

The Battle of the Big Hole, although fought with but a handful of men, was one of the most brilliant, heroic, and desperate pieces of work known in the annals of Indian warfare.

It was a glorious achievement, a victory dearly bought but gallantly won, and the grand old Seventh Infantry has no brighter page in its history than that earned by this day's work.

Gibbon's name will for ages to come be a terror to belligerent redskins, and Indian mothers will use that name to reduce to obedience their refractory offspring, long after he who rendered it illustrious shall have passed away.

The following is a list of the casualties that occurred in the action:

Seventh Infantry
Killed

Company A   Capt William Logan and Private John B Smith
Company B   First Lieut James H Bradley
Company D   Corporal William H Payne, Corporal Jacob Eisenhut, and Musician Francis Gallagher
Company E   Private Mathew Butterly
Company F   Privates William D Pomroy and James McGuire
Company G   First Sergeant Robert L Edgeworth, Sergeant William H Martin, Corporal Domminic O'Conner, Corporal Robert E Sale, and Privates John O'Brien and Gottlieb Mauz

Company H	Private McKindra L Drake (orderly for General Gibbon)
Company I	Sergeant Michael Hogan, Corporal Daniel McCaffrey, and Private Herman Broetz
Company K	First Sergeant Frederick Stortz, Musician Thomas Stinebaker, and Artificer John Kleis

Second Cavalry
Killed

Company L.	Sergeant Edward Page

Seventh Infantry
Wounded

	Col. John Gibbon, Seventh Infantry (left thigh, severe flesh wound).
Company A	First Lieut. C. A. Coolidge (both legs above knees, right hand, severe); Private James C. Lehmer (right leg, serious); Private Charles Alberts (under left breast, serious); Private Lorenzo D. Brown (right shoulder, serious); Private George Leher (scalp, slight).
Company D	Sergeant Patrick C. Daly (scalp, slight); Corporal John Murphy (right hip, severe); Musician Timothy Cronan (right shoulder and breast; serious); Private James Keys (right foot, severe).
Company E	Sergeant William Wright (scalp, slight); Sergeant James Bell (right shoulder, severe).
Company F.	Capt. Constant Williams (right side, severe, and scalp, slight); Sergeant William W. Watson (right hip, serious; died August 29, 1877); Corporal Christian Luttman (both legs, severe); Musician John Erikson (left arm, flesh); Private Edwin D. Hunter (right hand, severe); Private George Maurer (through both cheeks, serious); Private Charles B. Gould (left side, severe).

Company G.	Sergeant John W. H. Frederic (left shoulder, flesh); Sergeant Robert Benzinger (right breast, flesh); Private John J. Conner (right eye, slight); Private George Baughart (right shoulder, thigh, and wrist, severe); Private James Burk (right breast, serious); Private Charles H. Robbuke (left hip, slight).
Company I.	First Lieut. William L. English (through back, serious, and scalp, slight; died August 19, 1877); Corporal Richard M. Cunliffe (shoulder and arm, flesh); Private Patrick Fallon (hip and leg, serious); Private William Thompson (left shoulder, flesh); Private Joseph Daross (ankle and leg, serious).
Company K.	Second Lieut. C. A. Woodruff (both legs above knees, and left heel, severe); Sergeant Howard Clarke (heel, severe); Private David Heaton (right wrist, severe); Private Mathew Devine (forearm, serious); Private Philo O. Hurlburt (left shoulder, flesh).

Citizen Volunteers

Killed	L. C. Elliott, John Armstrong, David Morrow, Alvin Lockwood, Campbell Mitchell, H. S. Bostwick (post guide, Fort Shaw).
Wounded	Myron Lockwood, Otto Lyford, Jacob Baker, William Ryan.

Recapitulation

	Killed	Wounded
Officers Seventh Infantry	2	5[1]
Enlisted men Seventh Infantry	20	30[2]
Enlisted men Second Cavalry	1	1
Volunteers (citizens)	5	4
Bostwick (citizen)	1[3]	
Total	29	40

John Gibbon, Colonel Seventh Infantry
Commanding Dist. Montana
September 2, 1877

---

1. One officer since died.
2. One enlisted man since died.
3. Post guide at Fort Shaw.

The fact has been repeatedly stated, as showing the highly civilized condition of the Nez Percés, that they did not scalp or otherwise mutilate the bodies of the soldiers who fell within their lines. It is true they did not while the fight was in progress, probably owing to the good influence exerted over the warriors by Chief Joseph, who is, in reality, an Indian of remarkably high moral principles; but Lieutenant Van Orsdale writes, under date of January 4, 1889:

"About six weeks after the fight, I returned to the battle-ground to rebury our dead, many of them having been dug up by Indians, bears, and wolves; and, to destroy one more fiction which has obtained credence, to the effect that these Indians did not scalp their victims, I must state that both Captain Logan and Lieutenant Bradley, as well as several private soldiers, had been dug up and scalped, presumably by those Indians who had been left behind to care for the wounded hidden in the hills near there."

In his official report of the fight, General Gibbon says: "I desire to speak in the most commendatory terms of the conduct of both officers and men (with the exception of the two cowards who deserted the howitzer). With the exception of Captain Logan and Lieutenant Bradley, both of whom were killed very early in the action, every officer came under my personal observation at one time or another during the fight, and where all were so active, zealous, and courageous, not only in themselves fighting and in cheering on the men, but in prompt obedience to every order, I find it out of the question to make any discrimination, and will simply mention the names of those who were present in the battle. They were Capts. C. C. Rawn, Richard Comba, Geo. L. Browning, J. M. J. Sanno, Constant Williams (wounded twice), and William Logan (killed), First Lieutenants C. A. Coolidge (wounded three times), James H. Bradley (killed), J. W. Jacobs, regimental quartermaster, Allan H. Jackson, Geo. H. Wright, and William H. English (mortally wounded, and since dead), and Second Lieutenants C. A. Woodruff, acting adjutant (wounded three times), J. T. Van Orsdale, E. E. Harden, and Francis Woodbridge."

General Terry, speaking of this fight in his official report, says:

I think that no one can read this report from Colonel Gibbon without feelings of great admiration for him, for his officers, for his men, and for the citizen volunteers who fought with them; but with the admiration which their gallantry, resolution, and devotion excites, other feelings will mingle. There can be no doubt that had the troops under Colonel Gibbon's command numbered 300 men instead of 142, the Nez Percé war would have ended then and there. Had the Seventh Infantry been maintained at even the minimum strength of an efficient regiment, the six companies engaged would have been sufficient to accomplish the complete overthrow of the enemy. It is painful to contemplate the famous Seventh Infantry, a regiment whose history is interwoven with that of the country from the battle of New Orleans to the present hour, so attenuated that with more than half of its companies present it could take into action but 142 men. And it is equally painful to behold its colonel, recently a major-general and a distinguished corps commander, reduced to the necessity of fighting, rifle in hand, as a private soldier, and compelled by a sense of duty to lead a mere squad of men as a forlorn-hope against a savage enemy from whom defeat would have been destruction.

General Sheridan has this to say of it:

During the month of June the Nez Percé Indians made an outbreak in the Department of the Columbia, and when followed by United States troops, hastily collected by Gen. O. O. Howard, commanding the department, were driven eastward, and, about the middle of June, entered Montana Territory via the Lo Lo trail, committing some depredations by the way. Col. John Gibbon, commanding the district of Montana, at once took the field at the head of 146 men and thirty-four citizens, who joined as volunteers, and on the 11th of August attacked them near Big Hole Pass, Montana, and, after one of the most desperate engagements on record, in which both sides lost heavily, he succeeded in driving them from the field.

When it is borne in mind that the Indians outnumbered the troops and citizens who attacked them more than two to one, and were equally as well armed and equipped, the good conduct of Colonel Gibbon and his men will be appreciated.

And General Sherman comments officially on the fight in these words:

There was but a single regiment of infantry (Seventh) in all Montana, Col. John Gibbon commanding, distributed to five posts, four on the eastern border and one on the western, with two small companies, A and G, commanded by Captain Rawn, who were employed in building the new post at Missoula. It is near this place that the Lo Lo trail debouches into the Bitter Root Valley, the western settlement of Montana. Joseph had many personal acquaintances among the settlers, some of which are civilized Flat-heads, and he managed with Indian cunning to cause information to go ahead that he was bound for the buffalo country; that if permitted to go on unmolested he would do no damage; that he had no quarrel with the people of Montana, only with General Howard, etc.

Colonel Gibbon was then at Fort Shaw, but by the 27th of July he had drawn to him what few men could be spared from Benton and Baker, marched rapidly 150 miles to Missoula, then taking every man that could be spared from there, he started in pursuit with fifteen officers and 146 men (afterward increased by thirty-four citizens).

He overtook the enemy on a branch of Big Hole, or Wisdom River, surprised them at daybreak of August 9, and for a time had the Indians at his mercy; but their numbers so far exceeded his own that he, in turn, was compelled to seek cover in a point of timber, where he fought on the defensive till the Indians withdrew at 11 p.m. of the 10th.

Colonel Gibbon reports his loss at two officers, six citizens, and twenty-one enlisted men killed; five officers, four citizens, and thirty-one men wounded; and on the part of the enemy, eighty-three were buried on the field, 'and six dead were afterward found in a ravine at some distance away.' It is otherwise known that the Indians sustained a very heavy and nearly fatal loss in wounded in this fight, and could Colonel Gibbon have had another hundred men the Nez Percé war would have ended right there.

Some newspaper scribblers have accused General Gibbon of rashness in attacking the Nez Percés when he knew that their force outnumbered his own so largely. He has been censured for sacrificing the lives of a large number of men in an action where he could not reasonably hope for success. But so far as known, no army officer, no military scholar, in short, no one competent to judge of the merits of the case, has ever criticised his conduct adversely.

An old maxim, loved and quoted by all Indian fighters is, that the time to fight Indians is when they are found. In Indian campaigning, a stern chase is usually not only a long, but a severe and tedious one, and the case in point is no exception to the rule, save in that General Gibbon overtook the Indians much sooner than a retreating band is usually overtaken. Yet he had made a hard march. He had been ordered to intercept and strike the renegades. In obedience to this order, he had marched his command more than 250 miles, and now that he had overtaken the fugitives, must he go into camp, fortify himself, and calmly wait for reinforcements, or for the Indians to attack him? Had he done so, the Indians would of course have retreated so soon as they found that he had arrived in their neighbourhood. What would have been thought of such a course by his superiors? What would have been thought of it by these same pretentious newspaper critics? They would doubtless have raised the cry of cowardice as promptly as they raised that of rashness.

General Gibbon is not one of the kind of soldiers who stops to count hostile Indians under such circumstances as these. He fights them at sight, just as any other brave commander does, and takes the chances. His brilliant record in the civil war, as well as on the frontier, has long since convinced his superiors that he was made of this sort of material, and this is why he had so often been entrusted with commands in which he was required to exercise just this kind of generalship. While he is a cautious commander, within due and reasonable bounds, he is brave as a lion, and knows no such thing as disobedience of orders. He felt himself and his little army equal to a contest with the band of hostiles in his front, and the result proved that he was correct in his estimate.

The St. Paul *Pioneer Press* replied to an editorial which appeared in the New York *Herald*, soon after the fight, and written by one of these carpers, in these cogent terms:

> Both in its conception and execution, the plan of campaign followed by General Gibbon was a masterpiece of Indian fighting. Nothing can be further from the brilliant folly of Custer's dash than Gibbon's march and attack. It was wisely planned, and boldly carried out. The necessities of an Indian war are simple. They are to move swiftly, strike suddenly and hard, and to fight warily, but perseveringly and vigorously. All these things Gibbon did. He made a forced march, and completely surprised the enemy at the end of it. He fought the savages after their own fashion, retiring to cover after the first onset, and fighting singly, rifle in hand, officers and men alike, from the commander down, becoming sharpshooters for the time, and picking off the Indians like born frontiersmen. And the battle was a victory, a brilliant success, in that it inflicted a terrible punishment on the Nez Percés, strewed the valley with dead Indians, and sent the crippled remnant of the band fleeing to the mountains. General Gibbon is a shrewd and bold Indian fighter—and the *Herald* writer is an ass.

General Gibbon took into the action, six companies of infantry. Had these companies been maintained on a war-footing of 100 men each, as all companies and regiments should be, his force would have been 600 men, instead of less than 200. With such a force, he could easily have surrounded the Indians while they slept and have killed them all; but a pettifogging Congress had cut down the strength of the army to such an extent that the companies numbered less than twenty-five men each, and with this force Gibbon was unable to deal with the Indians as he could have done with a proper force. The fight was prolonged, and the loss of life was much heavier than it would have been with a suitable force of soldiers on the field, so that the Forty-third Congress, which first reduced the army to its present beggarly proportions, is morally responsible for many, if not all, of the lives lost and wounds received by the brave men who participated in that affair.

Although, owing to this insufficient force of men, the fight was not a complete victory for our troops, it was nevertheless a most stinging blow to the Nez Percés. They had never before engaged in a war with our soldiers, but Indian tradition and Indian gossip had told them that the pale-faced soldiers were slow riders, slow walkers, and poor fighters; that one Indian could whip five soldiers any day. But this fight proved to them the falsity of these stories. It taught them that even "walking soldiers" were swift pursuers, good hunters, and deadly assailants when led by a brave chief. It taught them that the white man could move by night; that while the Indian slept, the soldier crept; that his tread was so stealthy that even the lightest sleeper, the most watchful warrior, could not hear his approach, and that it was not safe for the red man to close his eyes while the white soldier was on his trail. It taught them that the foot soldiers were marksmen; that their bullets could search out the hiding-place of the wiliest

Indian in the mountains; that in the face of the deadliest fire the Indians could pour forth, they, the soldiers, could come into his camp, shoot him down, and burn his lodges. It taught him that one white soldier could whip two Indians; that the Indian's ability to skulk and hide were no match for the white man's courage. In short, it taught him that the Indian's only safety, when overtaken by soldiers, was in surrender or in flight, in reaching a hiding-place beyond the White Father's domain, and that the flight thither, in order to be successful, must be the most rapid that horses could make. It taught the Nez Percés a lesson they will never forget, and undoubtedly rendered their final capture a much easier and less costly affair than it otherwise would have been, if indeed it could else have been accomplished at all.

And the Nez Percés accepted the lesson so taught. So soon as their village was well out of the way of Gibbon's rifles, they started for the British Possessions, and though closely pursued by troops all the way, who thrice overtook and attacked them *en route*, they made no other stand until General Miles headed them off near Bear Paw Mountain in Northern Montana, and captured nearly all their horses. Then they were compelled to fight or surrender. They made a four days' fight, but it was a spiritless one, and finally succumbed to the inevitable, and laid down their arms.

It has for years been claimed, and repeatedly shown, that one white man was equal to three or four Indians in a fight, position and other things being equal, and rarely has any band of Indians been encountered who would willingly stand their ground and fight white men, either soldiers or citizens, unless certain that they outnumbered the whites to some such extent. But here was a body of

Nez Percés who stood bravely up against a force of nearly half their own numbers; who fought so desperately and so gallantly that the troops who assaulted them and at first put them to flight, were afterward compelled to fall back and take cover; who followed these troops; hemmed them in; advanced on them; harassed them with a deadly fire for twenty hours; only withdrawing when they had reason to believe that reinforcements for the troops were at hand.

Yet General Gibbon and his Spartan band of veterans attacked this superior force, charged into its midst, drove it from its camp in confusion, fought it hand-to-hand in the brush, and inflicted on it such a punishment as probably no command of equal numbers has ever before inflicted on Indians under similar conditions and in so short a time. Several of the veterans who were in this action, and who had fought Sioux Indians repeatedly, said afterward that they would rather fight five Sioux than one Nez Percé. It is, therefore, the highest possible tribute to Gibbon and his men, to record the fact that they were able to hold their ground for a day against such a force as this, and to kill and wound so many of them.

Eighty-nine dead Indians were found and buried on the field, nearly three times the number of men lost by General Gibbon, and it is known that a large number of mortally wounded warriors were carried away and hidden during the day and night that the soldiers never found. Ranchmen residing near the battle-field tell us that they find skeletons in the neighbouring forests every summer; some of them two or three miles away from the battle-ground; some of them hidden in gulches and among rocks and logs, which they suppose to be those of Indians killed in this fight, and who were doubtless carried away and concealed by their friends, or who, finding themselves mortally wounded, crawled hither and hid themselves to die in seclusion rather than have their bodies fall into the hands of the white men.

Besides, it is said that Joseph carried away with him a number who were so seriously wounded that they died on the trail. He is said to have admitted, after his final capture, that 208 of his people were killed in the Big Hole fight. If this be true, then there were a larger number of Indians killed than of white men engaged. It is a well-known fact, that only about one hundred warriors finally surrendered to General Miles, and that only about one hundred escaped to the British Possessions at the time of the surrender. Hence the conclusion seems just, that 200 or more must have been lost in the fight with Gibbon.

How skilfully General Gibbon planned his attack on the Nez Percés; how quietly and stealthily he moved his little army down Trail Creek and up along the side of the bluff; how carefully he formed it in line of battle within a stone's-throw of the hostile camp without alarming it, and all in the dead of night; how gallantly his men charged through the jungle, waded the river, swept through the camp dealing death to its fleeing occupants; how the men subsequently took and held their position in the mouth of Battle Gulch under the galling fire of these trained warriors, are facts which no one can properly realize and appreciate save those who were there.

But the battle-field tells its own mute story even now. As I walked over it and saw the hundreds of bullet marks on trees, rocks, and logs, and thought of the thousands of other missiles that entered the earth and left no abiding marks, I was impressed with the remarkable accuracy of the shooting done by the Indians. Nearly every tree and every object in the valley and in the mouth of Battle

Gulch capable of bearing a bullet mark is cut and scarred in a frightful manner, and some of the trees are literally girdled. Many of the *teepee* poles that still lie scattered over the river bottom have bullet holes through them, and thousands of empty cartridge-shells still lie scattered over the field, though it is said that thousands more have been carried away by relic hunters or trampled into the earth.

No true American can read the record of this light without feeling proud that he is an American; that he is a brother to the brave men who stood so nobly together under such an ordeal—an ordeal, in short, that will stand in history on a parallel with the charge of Balaklava or the battle of Bunker's Hill.

As an evidence of the severity of this fight, and of the courage displayed by the officers, attention is called to the fact that of the seventeen engaged, seven of them were hit fourteen times, as follows:

General Gibbon, thigh 1 Captain Williams, head and body 2 Captain Logan, head (killed) 1 Lieutenant Bradley, head (killed) 1 Lieutenant Coolidge, both hands and legs 3 Lieutenant English, head, wrist, and back (died of wounds) 3 Lieutenant Woodruff, both thighs and heel 3—Total 14

Chapter 6

Veterans of the civil war, and men who have been years on the frontier, who have participated in many of the most sanguine Indian campaigns ever fought, say this was the most hotly-contested field they were ever on. They tell us that never have they seen such cool and determined fighting, at such short range, kept up for so long a time, by Indians; that never have they known so many bullets placed with such deadly accuracy, and so few to fly wild as in this fight. Nearly every man engaged in the action, white or red, officer, private soldier, or citizen, seemed a cool, deliberate sharpshooter; and the fact that after the first assault both parties kept closely covered all day, alone accounts for the fact that so many survived the fiery ordeal. The Indians did splendid work and elicited from the beleaguered soldiers expressions of admiration for their marksmanship, as well as for their bravery and prowess in fierce, close work.

An old sergeant, who was with the Seventh at Gettysburg, when it aided so nobly in holding Little Round Top, says there was no hotter place on that historic hill than he found in the Big Hole on the 9th of August, 1877.

After the battle General Gibbon issued the following congratulatory order to his men:

Regimental Orders, No. 27
Headquarters
Seventh Infantry
Battle-Field of the Big Hole
Montana Territory
Aug. 11, 1877
The regimental commander congratulates the regiment upon the result of the conflict here with the hostile Nez Percés on the 9th and 10th inst. While mourning for the dead, Capt. William Logan and First Lieut. James H. Bradley and the twenty-one enlisted men, who fell gallantly doing a soldier's duty, we can not but congratulate ourselves that after a stern chase of over 250 miles, during which we twice crossed the rugged divide of the Rocky Mountains, we inflicted upon a more numerous enemy a heavier loss than our own, and held our ground until it gave up the field.

In respect to the memory of the gallant dead, the officers of the regiment will wear the usual badge of mourning for thirty days.

John Gibbon
Colonel Seventh Infantry, Commanding
Official: Levi F. Bennett
First Lieutenant and Adjutant Seventh Infantry

In this connection it is deemed proper to give the following facts in regard to General Gibbon's record as a soldier:

He was born in Pennsylvania and appointed to the Military Academy at West Point from North Carolina. Graduated July 1, 1847, brevet second lieutenant. He was commissioned a second lieutenant September 18, 1847. Served in the Mexican war and in the Seminole war in Florida. Promoted to first lieutenant September 12, 1850.

Served as instructor of artillery at West Point 1854 to 1859. Promoted to captain November 2, 1859. Served in Utah 1860-61. Was chief of artillery on General McDowell's staff, October, 1861, to May, 1862. Brigadier-general of volunteers May, 1862.

Was in the battles of Grangeville, Manasas, South Mountain, and Antietam. Brevetted major-general of volunteers for gallant and meritorious conduct at Antietam. He held an important command at the battle of Fredericksburg, where he was severely wounded. Was brevetted lieutenant-colonel U.S.A. for gallant and meritorious services at the battle of Fredericksburg. Was severely wounded at the battle of Gettysburg while commanding the Second Corps, and brevetted colonel U.S.A. for gallant and meritorious service in that action.

He also held an important and responsible command in the Richmond campaign, and was brevetted brigadier-general U.S.A. for gallant and meritorious services at Spotsylvania. Was commissioned major-general of volunteers June 7, 1864. Brevetted major-general U.S.A. for gallant and meritorious conduct in the capture of Petersburg. Mustered out of the volunteer service June 15, 1866, and commissioned a colonel U.S.A. July 28, 1866. Promoted to brigadier-general U.S.A. July 10, 1885, and appointed to the command of the district of the Rocky Mountains. He commanded the column that rescued Reno from the Sioux Indians in June, 1876.

An officer who has served with him several years, and knows him intimately, says:

He is an able writer and deep thinker, a thorough soldier, and no politician; honest, strict on duty, and genial and kind off duty. He is brave as a man can be in battle. A true and loving husband, a kind father, and the truest kind of a friend. A thorough sportsman, temperate, modest, and as careful of the welfare of the humblest enlisted man as of his chief of staff.

Capt. Constant Williams, in a private letter to the author, under date of December 23, 1888, says:

I wish to bear testimony of the noble bearing of General Gibbon during the whole time the fight was in progress, under the most trying circumstances. His coolness and utter indifference to danger were so marked, and so admirable, that I have ever since that day taken him as my model for a commander.

Yet, notwithstanding this long record of brilliant services and well-merited rewards; notwithstanding this great and good man has grown gray fighting his country's battles; notwithstanding he has acquired, by study and experience, a military education and training second to none ever acquired by an American, a man who was suddenly elevated from private life to the high office of Secretary of War has recently seen fit to publicly reprimand him for what he was pleased to term a disobedience of orders. The alleged offense consisted in General Gibbon's having pardoned a private soldier, who had been by court-martial convicted of a misdemeanour and imprisoned. He had served several months of his term, when General Gibbon, under whose orders the court-martial had been held, deeming him already sufficiently punished, issued a pardon and ordered him released. The One hundred and Twelfth Article of War expressly authorizes such action on the part of department commanders, but the Secretary of War, deeming his power greater than that which makes the laws, had previously issued an order forbidding commanding officers to issue pardons in such cases, and General Gibbon was accordingly severely reprimanded for a violation of this order. He appealed to the President, and that "Man of Destiny," ignoring the organic law of the land, approved the action of his Secretary.

Thus, a man who has rendered such distinguished services to his country as to merit the gratitude and reverence of every loyal American; a man who has spent the best years of his life in fighting his country's battles and in studying and obeying her laws, was insulted and degraded by men who, so far as true moral worth is concerned, are unworthy to sit at the same table with him.

Capt. William Logan entered the regular army before the beginning of the late war, and rose from the ranks through the successive grades of corporal, sergeant, second and first lieutenants. He was commissioned a captain October 4, 1878. He saw a great deal of active service during the civil war, and bore an excellent reputation as a brave soldier.

First Lieut. James H. Bradley had been in the army eleven years, during the greater portion of which time he had been in active service on the frontier; had participated in several Indian campaigns, and had repeatedly distinguished himself for coolness and bravery in the face of danger.

First Lieut. William L. English was commissioned a second lieutenant in the One-hundred and First Regiment, Illinois Volunteers, May 1, 1863. On March 5, 1864, he was promoted to a first lieutenancy, and mustered out of the volunteer service June 7, 1865. He was appointed a second lieutenant in the regular army June 18, 1867, and promoted to the rank of first lieutenant October 24, 1874. His record is also that of a brave and capable officer.

Of the other officers who participated in the fight and survived its dangers, the following facts will no doubt be of interest to the general public:

General Gibbon is now (February, 1888) in command of the Department of the Columbia, with headquarters at Vancouver Barracks, Washington.

Captain Comba is on recruiting service at Pittsburgh, Pa. He is within two files of the rank of major, and in the usual course of events will be promoted to that grade within a year or two.

Captain Sanno is stationed at Fort McKinney, Wyoming, and Captain Williams at Fort Laramie, Wyoming.

Captain Browning died in Paris, May 1, 1882, and Captain Rawn at Lancaster, Pa., October 6, 1887.

Lieutenant Coolidge was promoted to a captaincy, vice Logan, August 9, 1877, and is now stationed at Camp Pilot Butte, Wyoming.

Lieutenant Jacobs was promoted to a captaincy in the Quartermaster's Department, 1882, and is now stationed at Atlanta, Ga.

Lieutenant Jackson was made a captain November 14, 1885, and is now stationed at Fort Washakie, Wyoming.

Lieutenant Woodruff was promoted to a captaincy in the Subsistence Department for gallant and meritorious conduct in the battle of the Big Hole, and is now on duty at General Gibbon's headquarters, March, 1878.

Second Lieutenant Van Orsdale was promoted to first lieutenant August 20, 1877, and regimental quartermaster June 1, 1885, and is stationed at Fort Laramie, the present headquarters of the Seventh Regiment.

Lieutenant Harden is detailed at West Point as instructor in tactics.

Lieut. Francis Woodbridge is on indefinite leave of absence at Detroit, Mich., awaiting retirement on account of ill health.

Chapter 7

A grateful country has erected on the Big Hole battlefield a fitting monument, a modest but enduring shaft of solid granite, which marks the scene of the bloody conflict and tells in mute but eloquent words the story of the victory won there. The base of the monument is five feet six inches square; the pedestal is four feet six inches square by three feet seven inches in height, and the height of the entire structure is nine feet ten inches. On the north face of the shaft are carved the words:

Erected By the United States

On the east face the words:

On this field 17 officers and 138 men of the 7th U. S. Infantry, under its colonel, Bvt. Major-General John Gibbon, with 8 other soldiers and 36 citizens, surprised and fought all day a superior force of Nez Percé Indians, more than one-third of the command being killed and wounded.

On the south is inscribed:

To the officers and soldiers of the army, and citizens of Montana, who fell at big hole, August 9, 1877, in battle with Nez Percé Indians.

And on the west side is a list of the soldiers and citi-

THE MONUMENT ON THE BIG HOLE BATTLE-FIELD

zens killed in the action, which is the same as that already quoted from General Gibbon's report.

The stone was cut in Concord, N. H., shipped to Dillon, Mont., by rail, and hauled from there to the battlefield by ox teams. It was placed in position in September, 1883, by a detachment of soldiers from Fort Missoula, under command of Capt. J. P. Thompson, of the Third Infantry. It cost about $3,000, an appropriation of that amount having been made for the purpose by Congress.

General Howard followed the Nez Percés through the mountains, and learning that they had determined to take refuge in the British Possessions he sent a courier to General Miles, at Fort Keogh, who, taking the field at the head of six hundred men, headed off the fugitives at Bear Paw Mountains in Northern Montana, and captured them after a desultory fight lasting through four days.

Chief Joseph's reply to General Miles' demand for surrender is a curiosity in the way of Indian rhetoric. It is in these words:

"Tell General Howard I know his heart. What he told me before I have in my heart. I am tired of fighting. Our chiefs are killed. Looking Glass is dead. Too-hul-hul-sote is dead. The old men are all dead. It is the young men who say yes or no. He who led on the young men is dead. It is cold and we have no blankets. The little children are freezing to death. My people, some of them, have run away to the hills, and have no blankets, no food; no one knows where they are—perhaps freezing to death. I want to have time to look for my children and see how many of them I can find. Maybe I shall find them among the dead. Hear me, my chiefs. I am tired; my heart is sick and sad. From where the sun now stands I will fight no more forever."

As stated in Joseph's message, while the negotiations

for the surrender were in progress, White Bird, with a few of his followers, escaped through Miles' lines and fled to the north. They were not pursued, and succeeded in time in reaching Woody Mountain, in the Northwest Territory, where Sitting Bull and his band were encamped at the time. When the Sioux saw the Nez Percés coming, they supposed them to be their enemies, the Black Feet, and prepared to fight them, but White Bird halted when within a mile of the Sioux camp, sent in a runner to announce himself, and when the Sioux learned who their visitors were, they received them with open arms.

Major Walsh, of the Northwest mounted police, happened to be in Sitting Bull's camp at the time, and describes White Bird and his people as being the toughest looking party of Indians he had ever seen. Their horses were mere skin and bone; some of them scarcely able to walk. The Indians, men, women, and children, were half naked, some of them with hands and feet frozen, and they had not a pound of food of any kind with them.

Too-hul-hul-sote and Looking Glass were both killed in the fight with Miles.

White Bird is still living near Fort MacLeod, in the Northwest Territory, with his family and a few followers.

After the surrender, Joseph and a few of his retainers were sent to Fort Leavenworth, where they were imprisoned until July 21, 1878, at which time they were placed in charge of the Indian Bureau and located in the Indian Territory. In June, 1885, they were removed to the Colville Reservation, in Washington Territory, where they now live unrestrained. Joseph is hale, hearty, and cheerful, and has accumulated considerable wealth in the way of cattle and horses. He says he will never again go on the war path; that he has had enough of fighting pale-face soldiers; that their bravery is more than a match for the cunning and prowess of the red man.

And to Gibbon's command, more than to any and all others who pursued and fought Joseph and his men, belongs the honour of having broken the proud spirits of these dusky warriors; of having killed their best men; of having defeated them on their chosen field. To Gibbon and his brave men, in short, belong the laurels of the Nez Percé war of 1877.

Chief Joseph, the Nez Percé

by Edmond Stephen Meany

Preface

During the summer session of the University of Wisconsin in 1900 there was assigned to me for especial research and report, in the class in History of the West, the subject of Chief Joseph, the Nez Percé. Finding the material abundant, and knowing that this great Indian was still living on the Colville Reservation in my home state of Washington where he could be visited for the latest and unpublished information, it was decided to continue the study.

Most of the literature consulted was found in the libraries of the State Historical Society of Wisconsin and the University of Wisconsin. This information has been supplemented by numerous letters from and interviews with men who fought against Joseph and others who have known him intimately and by seven personal talks with the Chief at his home on the banks of the Nespilem River, Colville Reservation, Washington.

I have been greatly aided in this work by Professor P. J. Turner and the officers and attendants of the libraries mentioned, while my visit to the Chief was greatly facilitated by United States Senator A. G. Foster, Hon. W. A. Jones, United States Commissioner of Indian Affairs; Major Albert M. Anderson, agent and Henry M. Steele, sub-agent of the Colville Reservation; Barnett Stillwell, teacher of the Nespilem school; and the latter's little daughter Ada C. Stillwell, eleven years of age. This little girl having mingled with the Nez Percé children for four years has learned their language and acted as one of my interpreters.

Madison

Wisconsin

August, 1901

Chief Joseph, the Nez Percé

"Xenophon did no more than he." This was the emphatic language of Colonel Charles A. Coolidge when asked for his opinion of Chief Joseph. The Colonel, while a lieutenant in the Seventh Infantry under General Gibbon, fought against the Nez Percés and was thrice wounded in the Battle of the Big Hole.

He is hostile to civilization, and his handful of warriors are the most backward of all the tribes on the Colville Reservation, and, taking into consideration the fact that the Government has supplied them so lavishly with rations, clothing, and Implements for the past sixteen years, their condition should be very much different.[1] This is the opinion of one who has known Joseph and his people in no other relation than that of agency Indians. Between these two extreme views there lies a great volume of opinion of varying value and colour. In northern Idaho, northeastern Oregon and south-eastern Washington there are many people who remember the Indian outbreak of 1877. They claim that Joseph's people were

---

1. U. S. Commissioner of Indian Affairs, Annual Report, 1899, p.354. (Report by Albert M. Anderson, agent of the Colville Reservation).

cruel savages and that a mistake has been made in ascribing greatness of any kind to Chief Joseph. On the other hand, the military men, who fought Joseph and his band, and others who have studied the campaign, invariably give the Chief high rank for great and shrewd generalship.

It is the object of this study to examine all possible evidence that this product of American savagery may be more fairly Judged.

While contemplating the reports of the agents on the Reservation care should be exercised to retain an impartial point of view. Sitting Bull once exclaimed:

The Great Spirit made me an Indian but he did not make me an agency Indian![2]

C. E. S. Wood, who was with General Howard throughout the Nez Percé campaign, in speaking of another warrior, Poor Crane, Chief of the Cayuses, says that it would be as impossible for him to cultivate lands allotted to him in severalty as it would for a cougar to turn sheep-dog.[3] So it is largely with Joseph. The promises made to him at the time of his surrender were ruthlessly broken and for twenty four years he has been fed, clothed and otherwise treated practically as a prisoner of war. Joseph prefers his old familiar *tepee* to the rude, rough-board cabin built by the Government. He is a product of the wilderness. At the supreme hour in his life he showed that he possessed remarkable power. At the present time, a ward of the Government, he deports himself with a quiet and unassuming dignity which compels the respect of all who come in contact with him.

---

2. F. S. Drake: *Indian History* p.447; Maj. G. W. Baird, 'General Miles's Indian Campaigns,' Century Vol. XX, p.370.
3. Century, XLVI, 445.

CHAPTER 1

Legal Status of Joseph's Band
Before the War of 1877

It should be remembered that the Nez Percé nation is the largest federation of Indian tribes in the Pacific Northwest and that from the time that they first saw the white man, when the Lewis and Clark Expedition visited them in 1805, down to the present day it is a matter of pride with the nation at large that they have been the constant and unfailing friends of their pale-face brothers. This friendliness is commented on favourably in every published Journal of the early travellers who visited the Nez Percé country. As the white settlements multiplied and Territorial Governments were organized it became necessary, under the policy then in vogue, to make treaties with the Indians, to buy their lands and to fix the limits of their reservations. At this point started a misunderstanding with a comparatively small portion of the nation which finally culminated in the war of 1877.

When Washington Territory was created, by Act of Congress, dated March 2, 1853, its limits extended from the Pacific Ocean eastward to the Rocky Mountains, thus embracing the Nez Percé lands. In his first message to the legislature,[1] Governor Isaac I. Stevens recommended that Congress be memorialized to provide for quieting Indian titles to the lands of the Territory. This was done, Congress acted promptly and on June 11, 1855, the Nez Percé Indians concluded their first treaty with the white men.

Here again we find evidence of the Nez Percé friendship for the whites. The council grounds were near the present City of Walla Walla. Besides the Nez Percés there were assembled for the same purposes the Cayuses, Walla Wallas, Umatillas, Yakimas and other smaller tribes. Six thousand Indians were in council with sixty whites. Yellow Serpent, Chief of the Cayuses, arranged for a massacre of the whites. This was prevented by Lawyer, the powerful head chief of the Nez Percés, who informed Governor Stevens, the white Tyer, of his danger, moved his *tepee* into the camp of the whites and averted danger after which the treaties with all the tribes were promptly concluded.[2]

In this first Nez Percé treaty is found the cause of all the trouble with these uniformly friendly Indians. The difficulty lay in fixing the bounds of the proposed reservation for the Nez Percés and especially, in subsequent adjustments, to determine whether Wallowa Valley the ancient home of Joseph's tribe was or was not included in the lands ceded by the Indians to the whites.

Two years after the war there appeared in the *North American Review*[3] an article purporting to come from Chief Joseph in which he describes the death scene of his father (also known as Chief Joseph) in which the father cautions the son who is about to succeed him as chief to

1. *Washington Territorial Honor Journal*, 1854, pp.15-22.
2. Hazard Stevens, Life of Isaac I. Stevens, Vol.11, jg.47.
3. Vol. CXXVIII, pp.412-433.

always remember that his father never sold his country.[4] To this article General O. O. Howard replied[5] giving his view of the Wallowa campaign and calling especial attention to the fact that Chief Joseph had sold his country as his name was the third on the list of Indian signatures to the treaty of 1855.

In the matter of that signature, General Howard was correct.[6] But while it is true that Joseph's father signed that treaty in 1855 it is not true that by doing so he sold his beloved Valley of Winding Waters. Nearly four years lapsed between the conclusion of the treaty of 1855 and its ratification by the Senate. When the news of that ratification reached Washington Territory, United States Indian Agent A. J. Cain hastened to meet the Nez Percés in a council at Weipe, the root grounds of the tribes.

Among the chiefs assembled were the older Joseph, Looking Glass and White Bird. Each one spoke his joy that the treaty had been approved. Among other things Joseph said:

> The line was made as I wanted it; not for me, but my children that will follow me; there is where I live, and there is where I want to leave my body. The land on the other side of the line is what we gave to the great father.[7]

Mr. Cain, representing his government, said he was especially pleased to hear Joseph and these other Indian Chiefs speak so approvingly of this treaty. Then came the point of departure. The Government failed to keep the

4. Ibid. p.419.
5. Ibid. Vol. CXXIX, pp.53-64.
6. See pamphlet edition of the treaty published at the time of its proclamation, April 29, 1859.
7. United States Commissioner of Indian Affairs, *Annual Report*, 1859, pp.418-423.

promises of the treaty. White settlers increased. Gold was discovered in the Nez Percé country, in 1860, causing a rush of white and Chinese prospectors and miners. They brought whiskey among the Indians to the disgust of some of the chiefs.[8] The mining town of Oro Pino was established on the reservation, about ninety miles from the agency.[9]

Attempts were made to construe the treaty of 1855 as having ceded to the whites the Wallowa and Imnaha and other valleys which were held by the bands or tribes of Joseph, Looking Glass, White Bird and Too-hul-hul-sote. These chiefs rebelled against such construction and became known as the non-treaty Nez Percés. They taunted the other bands, or treaty Indians, with the fact that the promised supplies and improvements never came from the Government. This argument was silenced for a time when the first supplies came in 1861 and 1862 but it broke out with fresh vigour when the supplies were shut off again.[10]

All through such, evidences of bad faith the bulk of the Nez Percé nation remained friendly while the non-treaty Indians remained off the reservation, refused all supplies and spent their time on the lands they claimed as homes or in the buffalo country east of the Rocky Mountains. In order to settle the vexed question of the title to the Wallowa Valley and other disputed lands a commission was appointed to meet the Nez Percés at Lapwai in 1863. The treaty was concluded on June 9th and was signed by Chief Lawyer and fifty other chiefs and headmen. This treaty was not ratified by the Senate until April 17, 1867. It was soon found that this treaty was incomplete, so three

---

8. Ibid.,1866, pp.193-194.
9. Ibid., p.193.
10. United States Commissioner of Indian Affairs, *Annual Report*, 1865, pp. 236-237.

chiefs—Lawyer, Timothy and Jason—were taken to Washington City where they concluded, on August 13, 1868, a supplemental treaty which was ratified by the Senate on February 16, 1869.

Chief Joseph and the other non-treaty Indians voted against these two treaties but, as General Howard says[11] the Government decided that the decision of a majority of the Nez Percés should bind them all and the reservation was accordingly cut down so as to throw open to settlement by the whites the Wallowa and other valleys claimed by the non-treaty Nez Percés.

On this question of a majority of Indians binding a minority C. E. S. Wood[12] says it is applying North American politics to the North Americans who never heard of such a thing as one man binding another without his consent.

If you consider a convention of Indians bound by rules and customs they never heard of and repudiate as soon as stated, then this was 'just.' If you consider that the consenting chiefs were not affected to a spear of grass, while the non-consenting were utterly uprooted in their promised district and conveyed wholly to a different one then perhaps you'll agree with young Joseph's simile:

A man wants to buy my horses. I refuse to sell them.

He goes to my neighbour and says: "Joseph has fine horses. I want them but he will not sell them."

My neighbour says: "I will sell them to you."

So he comes back to me and says: "Joseph I have bought your horses."[13]

---

11. In a personal letter dated at Burlington, Vermont, July 24, 1900.

12. In a personal letter dated at Portland Oregon, July 23, 1900.

13. See, also, 'Young Joseph, An Indian's View of Indian Affairs,' *North American Review*, Vol. CXXVIII, 419-420.

Acting under instructions from the Interior Department, T. B. Odeneal, Superintendent of Indian Affairs in Oregon, and John B. Monteith, agent of the Nez Percé Reservation, held a council at Lapwai with young Joseph and his band on March 27, 1873. These commissioners submitted a report to the Interior Department to the effect that the Wallowa Valley was the ancient home of Joseph's people and had never been rightly ceded to the United States. Acting on this report the Secretary of the Interior gave orders that the band of Indians be notified that they could continue to occupy that Valley in peace. Immediately following this President Grant issued an executive order dated June 16, 1873, withdrawing the Wallowa Valley from settlement and setting it aside as a reservation for the roaming Nez Percé Indians.[14]

This executive order displeased the people of Oregon and Governor L. P. Grover wrote a long letter in July, 1873, to the Government asking that the order be revoked, the Wallowa Valley restored to settlement and the Indians removed to the Idaho reservation.[15] Evidently the Oregon move had its effect for on June 10, 1875, President Grant issued another executive order annulling the former one and throwing the Wallowa Valley open to settlement again.[16] Thus Joseph's band after enjoying those two years of acknowledged freedom in his old home valley was again given to understand that the white man had a better right there than he.

It is thus seen that Joseph's band could legally be bound by only one treaty, the first one in 1855, which gave the

14. Col. H. Clay Wood, Asst. Adj. Gen. Dep. of the Columbia to Brig. Gen. O. O. Howard, *Report on Status of Young Joseph*, p.33, Indian Pamphlet, Vol. XXXVIII, Wisconsin State Historical Society; U.S. Secretary of War, *Annual Report*, 1876-77, pp. 88-99.
15. General O. O. Howard, *Nez Percé Joseph*, pp.25-27.
16. Wood, *Status of Joseph*, p. 34.

Indians an immense reservation including Joseph's Wallowa Valley.[17] To all other treaties they refused assent. The methods employed by the Government to take away those lands would puzzle a wiser head than Joseph's and it certainly seems shameful that the Government should use its might to settle a dispute with people who had been such constant friends as had the Nez Percés.[18]

---

17. Howard, *Nez Percé Joseph*, p.7.
18. Ibid., p. 27; Wood, *Status of Joseph*, supplemental report.

CHAPTER 2

Negotiations and Troubles
Preceding the Outbreak

The exhaustive report by Colonel H. Clay Wood to
General O. O. Howard on the Status of Young Joseph and
his band was dated January 8, 1976. In forwarding a copy
of that report to the Government, General Howard asked
that a commission be appointed to confer with these dis-
affected Indians and on October 18, 1876, the. Interior
Department designated the following as the Nez Percé
Indian Commissioners: D. H. Jerome of Saginaw, Michi-
gan, Chairman; Brigadier General O. O. Howard, Major
H. Clay Wood, William Stickney of Washington City; A. C.
Barstow, of Providence, Rhode Island.

In the meantime Major Wood, who had become greatly interested in the band of Chief Joseph, arranged a conference with them about the middle of July, 1876. He was
accompanied on this errand by Colonel David Perry, First
Cavalry, commanding at Port Lapwai; Assistant Surgeon
Jenkins A. Fitzgerald, United States Army; and Lieutenant
Colonel William R. Parnell, First Cavalry.

They found the Indians greatly incensed over the killing of a member of their band on June twenty third by a
white man named Finlay.[1] Promises were made that the

white man should be arrested and tried for the crime. This was actually done later but the white man was acquitted.

On this same occasion a second conference was held at Port Lapwai on July twenty third when Ollicutt, Joseph's brother and himself a chief, produced an Indian map showing the lands they proposed to hold. This map included the Wallowa, Grande Ronde and Imnaha Valleys. They had not before claimed the Grande Ronde Valley. The conferences resulted in increasing Major Wood's respect for the justice of the claims of Joseph and his band. He also urged the appointment of an official commission which was done, as already stated, in October of that year.

The net results of the work of this commission may be said to consist simply of a restatement of the validity of Joseph's claim to the Wallowa Valley coupled with recommendations that since there are too many settlers already in that Valley that, by peaceful means if possible or by forceful means if necessary, Joseph's band should be transferred to some other reservation and that they be recompensed for the loss of the Wallowa Valley by giving them houses, fences, farm Implements and pasturage. The Commission could not make a treaty as the Indians declined to enter into any negotiations looking to that end.[2] The matter was left with the understanding that if the Indians committed any depredations they were to be forcibly put upon the Nez Percé Reservation in Idaho.

Early in January, 1877, Agent Monteith at Lapwai received instructions from the Interior Department, based on the recommendations of the commission. He sought to persuade the non-treaty Indians to come to the reservation. A little later General Howard received word that

1. Newspaper clipping in *Indian Pamphlet*, Vol. XXXVIII, Wisconsin State Historical Society: Howard, *Nez Percé Joseph*, p.32.
2. Howard, *Nez Percé Joseph*, p.65.

young Joseph wished to meet him at the Umatilla agency, alleging that the interpreters at Lapwai had not told his desires correctly to the Commission. General Howard sent his *aide-de-camp*, Lieutenant Boyle and Joseph, being ill, sent his brother Ollicutt. The outcome was a request to meet General Howard at Walla Walla. The General consented and on April nineteenth he was at Walla Walla where he also met Ollicutt, Chief Joseph being still too ill to attend the meeting. The talk did not amount to much except securing from General Howard a promise to meet at Lapwai in twelve days the Indians of Joseph's band and those of the Salmon River and other non-treaty tribes.

On May 3, General Howard was at Lapwai to keep his appointment. Joseph and his brother Ollicutt were there with about fifty of their band. The first day's talk amounted to little as the two brothers claimed that Chief White Bird and his band were coming on the following day to join in the council. General Howard and Agent Monteith were very careful to inform the Indians that they could do nothing but obey the Government. Their instructions were read and interpreted to the Indians who were told that if they would at once come onto the reservation they could have their pick of whatever lands were left.

On the following day White Bird and part of his band and Too-hul-hul-sote and part of his band came into the camp. The arrangement of the Indians for this council shows in what relative rank they probably held each other. Joseph sat on a low bench. Ollicutt half reclined on the ground at his feet and White Bird was just behind Joseph and a little to the left of Ollicutt. The Indians talked against the treaty by which their lands had been given away by others. The main spokesman was Too-hul-hul-sote who continually repeated phrases about the earth being his mother. Joseph finally asked for a postponement and General Howard wishing to call in more troops suggested that the Indians take plenty of time to think it all over. They would meet again on Monday. That would give three precious days to call in troops from Grande Ronde, Walla Walla and other neighbouring points.

On Monday, May seventh, the third interview took place. The Indians had received many accessions but none of the new troops had arrived. Again the Indians put forward as their spokesman the old "Dreamer", Chief Too-hul-hul-sote, who continued his talk about the earth and its sacredness to the Indian. The others seemed more restless. Some of them were armed and General Howard says[3] that he knew the crisis had come for him to prevent a possible massacre by a show of boldness. He consequently placed Too-hul-hul-sote under arrest and the other Indians almost immediately showed better temper.

The next day, as agreed, Chiefs Joseph, White Bird and Looking Glass rode out over the reservation with General Howard to pick out possible homes for their people. On Wednesday they examined another portion of the reservation. Each chief picked out the portion of the reservation he wanted. Captain Trimble's company of the First Cavalry had arrived and news had been received that two other companies, Whipple's and Winter's had arrived at the banks of the Grande Ronde. Joseph heard this last news and hurried matters to a settlement. All agreed to come onto the reservation in thirty days or about June fourteenth.

General Howard returned to Portland, Oregon, where he was soon after joined by Colonel E. C. Watkins, Inspector of Indian Affairs, who was to make a tour of the

---

3. Howard, *Nez Percé Joseph*, p.65.

agencies in General Howard's military Department of the Columbia, jokingly called because of its wide expanse, the "Geographical" Department. On May thirtieth, they started on this tour and by way of precaution, assembled the various renegade tribes along the Columbia for a council at Port Simcoe. This was a complete success, all the tribes promising to make peaceful settlements on reservations. They continued on to Lapwai and arriving there the very day the non-treaty Indians promised to be on the reservation the peace and quietness was disturbed by the receipt of a letter from Mount Idaho, dated June 14th., stating that sixty lodges of White Bird's and Joseph's Indians were placed at the head of Rocky Canyon, eight miles from there. The Indians were saucy and were buying arms and ammunition. They claimed that they would fight the soldiers when they came to force them onto the reservation.

Colonel Perry sent a small detachment of soldiers to see what was the trouble with the Indians. About noon these soldiers returned with two excited Indians whom they had met. These Indians brought the news that three or four Indians had committed a murder near State Creek, where there was a scattered settlement about forty miles beyond Mount Idaho. This information proved true. It was the beginning of hostilities.[4] Chief Joseph claimed that he knew nothing of this outbreak. He was away across the rim killing some beef for his wife who was ill, but he could do nothing else except continue with his people for the whites would never believe his story that he had really been in favour of peace and had intended to go onto the reservation.[5] After the murder of Richard Devine, the first victim of this war, on June thir-

4. General Nelson A. Miles, *Personal Recollections*, p.260; Howard, *Nez Percé Joseph*, p.92.
5. C. B. S. Wood, 'Chief Joseph, the Nez Percé,' *Century*, Vol. VI, 136.

teenth, three others—Henry Elfers, Robert Bland, and Henry Beckroge—were killed on the morning of June fourteenth. This stirred the Indians into a war fever. After a few hours of deliberation and peace talk,-Chief Joseph was also drawn to the side of war.

There followed a brief season of murder and outrage over the Camas Prairie, around Salmon River settlements and in the vicinity of Mount Idaho, to which village the settlers hastened for shelter. In all twenty one whites were murdered in this preliminary outbreak. Messengers were hastily sent to Fort Lapwai and preparations were at once made to check the Indians in their murderous forays.

CHAPTER 3

Skirmishes and Battles in Idaho

The first battle of the war was a decided victory for the Indians. They set a trap for the soldiers and at the proper moment it was sprung with disastrous results. The Nez Percés had never been at war with the whites. No one was sure of just how they would behave under fire. This first battle was convincing both as to their determination and ability to fight.

As already stated disquieting news came as a surprise from Mount Idaho to the small garrison at Fort Lapwai on June fourteenth, the very day these non-treaty Indians promised to be on the reservation. The next morning this news was followed by reports of the first murders. There was no delay at the garrison. It was instantly decided that an immediate attack must be made if those murders and outrages were to be checked. By evening of that same day Colonel Perry, commanding at the fort was on the march with every man available from his two skeleton companies of cavalry. In all officers and men they numbered but ninety men. At Grangeville, a small hamlet not far from Mount Idaho, the command was joined by about ten citizen volunteers.

At dawn the next day they were at the head of the canyon of White Bird Creek, at the bottom of which was the camp of the hostiles in plain view. The Indians had their pickets posted and Chief Joseph was noticed to send a messenger running to the camp from his position among the rocks. The messenger was observed to quietly awaken one of the chiefs and soon he returned with a white man's field glass. Now began active preparations for the engagement. The soldiers began the descent and the Indians leaving their women and non-combatants in the camp ascended the ravines to meet their enemies. They soon turned the flanks of the cavalry and precipitated the small body of troops into a retreat that became a rout. Colonel Perry in the evening sent a hasty report to General Howard saying that he had succeeded in rallying the remnant of his command at the head of the canyon and the Indians pursued in a running fight as far as Grangeville when they returned to White Bird Creek. One third of the whites were killed in this battle.

General Howard, who apparently by chance was at Fort Lapwai, was not idle. While Colonel Perry prepared for his march against the hostiles, the General sent couriers to the nearest telegraph line at Walla Walla. Captain Wilkinson made the long ride of one hundred and ten miles in the night arriving there at eight o'clock the next morning. General Howard tells us[1] that the dispatches thus hurried to the outside world called for the men under Colonel Whipple near the Wallowa Valley, and also all the available men from Vancouver, Stevens, Canby, Townsend, Klamath and Harvey. By the twenty first of June eight new companies had arrived at Lapwai. But they were small companies. In all the available force amounted to a few over two hundred men including a company of a little over twenty volunteers from Walla Walla under Captain Paige. On June twenty second this command marched out of the Fort at noon.

---

1. Howard, *Nez Percé Joseph*, pp.120-121.

Sunday, June twenty fourth, was spent in camp at Morton's ranch. This gave rise to many newspaper complaints to the effect that General Howard spent the precious time in giving religious exhortation and distributing Bibles to the men. The General claims that he needed that time to learn the whereabouts of the Indians, to give Captain Trimble's men time to get around to State Creek and to allow some additional troops to reach him from Lewiston. The next day the command marched to White Bird Creek being joined on the way by the remnant of Colonel Perry's command. The Indians had been reported still at their camp on White Bird Creek. Careful approach was made and soon it was found that the Indians had crossed the swift Salmon River. The dead of Perry's battle were buried and on the next day while preparing to cross the Salmon River a number of Joseph's Indians came dashing down the banks with a show of bravado. A long distance rifle fire was maintained against them with no effect except to drive the Indians back to the hills.

Hearing that men from the camp of Chief Looking Glass at the forks of the Clearwater were joining the hostiles, General Howard sent Colonel Whipple with the cavalry and the two Gatling guns to capture that chief with his band and turn them over as prisoners to the volunteer organizations at Mount Idaho. Whipple was joined by twenty volunteer citizens under command of Captain Randall. They arrived at the camp of Looking Glass at sunrise of July first. The chief at first agreed to surrender but later defiantly refused, resulting in an attack, in which several Indians were killed. The camp with a large amount of supplies and seven hundred and twenty five ponies were captured. Of course this added another tribe to the camp of the hostiles.

General Howard with part of his troops and Captain Trimble's men with volunteers under Hunter and McConville pushed down along the Snake in pursuit of Joseph who again crossed that river at Craig's Perry and proceeded back over the Camas Prairie region again. This move had been suspected, for Whipple's command had been ordered to Norton's ranch to wait there for Perry coming up with supplies from Port Lapwai. Whipple sent Scouts Poster and Blewett toward Craig's Perry where Joseph was likely to cross the Salmon river. Poster soon returned reporting Indians in force. They had fired on him and he had lost sight of his comrade. Lieutenant S. M. Rains with ten men and Scout Poster were sent out to ascertain the strength of the enemy. Whipple at once moved his whole command and soon quickened pace at the sound of firing. The Indians re-treated and it was found that Lieutenant Rains and every man of his little company had been killed.

On July fourth Whipple went out to give safer escort to Perry with the supply train. This was accomplished and a little later their camp at the Cottonwood, or Norton's ranch, was surrounded by Indians who made frantic efforts to dislodge the troops. Every man was on the line, in rifle pits, until sundown when the Indians withdrew for the night.

The next day, July fifth, Captain Randall's company of volunteers, numbering seventeen men, was attacked about two miles from the Cottonwood camp. When relief reached them it was found that Captain Randall was mortally wounded, one man killed and two others wounded. The Indians were driven off. Colonel Perry was charged with criminal delay in sending relief but a court of inquiry afterwards exonerated him.

General Howard instead of crossing the Salmon River when Joseph did pushed back toward Grangeville and prepared to engage the hostiles in a battle near the Clearwater. In this he was successful. Joseph was flushed with victory and quite willing to give open battle. There followed on July eleventh and twelfth the two days[1] engagement known as the Battle of the Clearwater. In the first day's fighting the forces were just about equal. On the second day there approached a supply train escorted by Jackson's cavalry company. Before the battle Joseph had placed his camp in security and crossed the river for a fair and open fight. The struggle was a serious one. The whites showed much dash and gallantry. The Indians Showed most remarkable marksmanship. The whites had put into the engagement four hundred fighting men and the Indians had over three hundred warriors who were assisted by the women bringing up spare horses and ammunition. The Indians lost twenty-three killed, forty wounded, many of whom afterwards died, and about forty prisoners. The whites lost thirteen killed and twenty-two wounded.

The Indians were finally routed and the cavalry began a hot pursuit. The Indians deserted their camp where food was found still cooking, showing that defeat had not been expected.

On the morning of the thirteenth the Indians were found across the Clearwater about a mile above the ferry at Kamiah. From this camp they watched every move of the whites. Perry's and Whipple's men passing near the enemy's crossing experienced a small skirmish without result except that the whites jumped from their horses and ran to cover. General Howard sought to throw a column around to the rear of the Indians' camp but the move was detected and the whole camp of hostiles began a retreat in earnest moving out over the Lo Lo Trail toward Montana.

CHAPTER 4
The Lo Lo Trail

This famous old trail was a well beaten Indian Highway over which the tribes had travelled for years before they had seen the first white men. It was their road to the buffalo country east of the Rockies. Many of the early travellers from Lewis and Clark[1] down mention the Lo Lo Trail. It was over this familiar highway that the Indians now began their memorable retreat.

General Howard had two plans of action before him. One was to leave a small garrison at Kamiah, go back to Lewiston, pick up supplies and press on to Missonla, Montana, leaving Camas Prairie and the harried Idaho country to the care of Colonel Green who would arrive from Boise, Idaho, in about ten days and to General Wheaton, who was hurrying on with the Second Infantry from Georgia. The second and approved plan was to form two columns and a reserve. General Howard would accompany the right column on a direct pursuit, General Wheaton should take the left column by way of the Mullan road to keep the renegade Columbia Indians pacified and the reserve, under Colonel Green, was to watch all trails and keep peace in the lately disturbed area.

---

1. Elliot Coues, *History of the Lewis and Clark Expedition*, Vol. II p.590.

These arrangements completed, a start was made on Thursday July twenty sixth. On Saturday General Howard, with McConville's volunteers made a reconnaissance to Little Camas, finding no signs of the Indian camps. On that day Major Sanford arrived from Colonel Green's command bringing three companies of cavalry under Bendire, Carr and Wagner and twenty Bannock scouts.

The trail so familiar to the Indians was a rough one for the troops who must take with them their few pieces of artillery and all their supplies and baggage. They had few extra horses while the Indians took with them about two thousand ponies. Patches of blood and hair on the logs that cumbered the trail told how the Indians had rushed on over the obstructions.

When Joseph started his retreat over the Lo Lo Trail dispatches were sent in all haste to the east. General John Gibbon, commanding in Montana at once began a march to intercept the hostiles. He left Port Shaw with every available man which made a little army of eight officers and seventy-six men, on his way to Fort Missonla one hundred and fifty miles away.[2]

Fort Missonla was occupied by two companies, Rawn's and Logan's. Hearing that Joseph was coming through Lo Lo Pass, Rawn took his command to that point, arriving there on July twenty fifth, accompanied by a number of citizen volunteers. They built up hasty fortifications in the narrow pass and none too soon for two days later the hostiles appeared. Under a flag of truce Chief Joseph had a talk with Captain Rawn, saying he had no quarrel with the people of Montana and simply wished to be allowed to pass on. Captain Rawn told him his people could not

2. Brig. Gen. John Gibbon, 'Battle of the Big Hole,' *Harper's Weekly*, Dec.21,1895, p.1215.

pass into the Bitter Root Valley unless they laid down their arms. On the next day negotiations were renewed and finding Captain Rawn determined Joseph said he would pass if he had to force his way. On the next morning firing was heard on the skirmish line. It looked like a serious moment but ere long it was found that Joseph had skilfully passed his whole band with their ponies and baggage over the mountain on the flank of Rawn's fortifications.[3] Most of the citizen volunteers had urged Rawn not to engage the Indians in a battle for that would surely mean that the victorious Indians would leave a trail of blood and ashes in the Bitter Root Valley. Rawn's little command later came up with the Indians strongly encamped in the Bitter Root Valley. It would have been folly to attack them with his few men so he returned to Port Missonla.

Colonel Charles A. Coolidge of the Seventh Infantry, United States Army, was a lieutenant in Logan's company of the same regiment during the Lo Lo Pass engagement. On June eighteenth last Colonel Coolidge was in Seattle, Washington, having but recently returned from the campaign in China. He is probably the only surviving officer of those present at Lo Lo Pass in July of 1877. He was later thrice wounded in the Battle of the Big Hole on August 9, 1877. In conversation with the writer, during his visit at Seattle, Colonel Coolidge said he thought that Rawn's handful of men at Lo Lo Pass manifested more "sand" and bravery than was shown even in the bloody and hard fought Battle of the Big Hole.

---

3. G. O. Shields, Battle of the Big Hole, p. 21.

CHAPTER 5

Battle of the Big Hole

As already stated General Gibbon had left Fort Shaw with all the available men on June twenty seventh. On arriving at Fort Missonla he was soon after joined by Rawn's and Logan's companies and Browning's company of infantry which had been ordered from Fort Ellis to Missonla. On August fourteenth General Gibbon left Fort Missonla to chase and attack Joseph's band. His command now numbered fifteen officers and one hundred and forty-six men. At this time the hostiles had about two hundred and sixty warriors, a large number of women and children and a great herd of ponies.

To get to Ross Hole it was necessary to cross a spur of mountains. At the foot of this spur stood Lockwood's ranch. The house was found thoroughly gutted. It was the only evidence of such depredation found in the Bitter Root Valley. Lockwood joined the forces and was severely wounded in the battle that followed. General Gibbon remarks that he thinks the demolition of Lockwood's home was done by stragglers, the pest of all armies, civilized or savage.[1] After crossing that spur of mountains it was necessary to cross the main divide before coming

1. General Gibbon, Battle of Big Hole, *Harper's Weekly*, Dec. 21, 1895, p.1216.

up with the retreating Indians. On the eighth of August the scouts located the Indians encamped on the banks of Ruby Creek, a tributary of the Big Hole River. Indian women were seen in the timber collecting lodge poles. Evidently the camp was to remain there for some time. Great caution was observed. The troops were quietly brought to the opposite side of the Creek during the night. One of the Indians started out to look after the herds early in the morning. As he was passing through the line of troops he was shot down. The first shot was the signal agreed upon for the assault so the charge was made upon the sleeping camp. Joseph, himself, acknowledges[2] that he was surprised but he claims that they thought, when Captain Rawn retired after the Lo Lo Pass engagement, that the Montana soldiers had decided to let them pass in peace.

The troops charged through the camp and began to set the *tepees* on fire. The warriors rallied, they gathered up their herds, took them to a safe place, the fighting men were hastily mounted and returned to the fight in a frenzy of anger. The soldiers were driven from the camp. General Howard was seriously wounded but continued to direct the fight with a rifle in his hand obtaining needed protection in a point of timber where the soldiers were finally held at bay by the Indians. The howitzer was captured by the Indians as it was approaching the battlefield. They destroyed it after the sergeant in charge had scattered the ammunition. Surrounded by Indians the soldiers kept up the fight all day. They had no provisions. Only four horses had been taken into the fight. One of these, Lieutenant Woodruff's, was killed by the

'An Indian's Views of Indian Affairs,' *North American Review*, .425-427.

Indians within the lines of the soldiers' camp. It supplied the only food the men had for over twenty-four hours.

During the day the soldiers were treated to a piece of tactics they did not relish but which they recognized as the actual practice of what the Nez Percés had shown them in a sham battle at Port Shaw the year before. The grass in the ravine leading up to the timber was set on fire. The Indians followed behind the blaze and smoke hoping to rush through for a final charge as the fire would drive the men from cover. In this case the wind changed just in time to blow the smoke and fire back from the timber shelter of the troops.

A night attack was expected but did not materialize.

The next day most of the Indians had gone but a few bands lingered around to do what damage they could. Twenty-five men volunteered under Captain Browing and Lieutenants Wright and Van Orsdale to go in search of the supply train, which they brought in at sundown much to the relief of the men. That second night vigilance again saved the command for at eleven o'clock a parting volley was fired into the camp and the Indians withdrew.

The next morning, August eleventh, parties were sent to bury the dead. The troops lost thirty-one killed and thirty-eight wounded. Eighty nine dead Indians were found on the field. Later the settlers reported finding human skeletons around the rocks and logs of that vicinity. These may have been the bones of wounded Indians who crawled away from the battlefield to die.[3] The whites buried the Indian dead as well as their own. The State of Montana has since erected on the battlefield a monument to the memory of the officers, soldiers and citizens who fell in that engagement.

3. G. O. Shields, *Battle of the Big Hole,* p .101.

The Indian dead included women and children. The Indians complained of this and Joseph also used strong language later in referring to the same thing.[4] It is difficult to see how the women and children could have been spared in that early morning raid on the camp. None such were wittingly killed unless they were caught shooting the soldiers as was several times the case. While visiting Chief Joseph and the remnant of his band on the Colville Reservation in June, 1901, the writer was told of an Indian women now seventy-one years of age, named Ta-ha-ya-ya. At the Battle of the Big Hole she was shot through the legs but in some way mounted a pony and fought like a demon by the side of the bravest warriors. Chief Joseph in telling of this woman went through motions to show how she was wounded, how her legs dangled from the saddle and how she fought. Surely soldiers could not be blamed for killing such a woman as this. Ta-ha-ya-ya is still alive and enjoys a great reputation among the Nez Percés. She was away on a visit among friends at Lapwai during the writer's visit at Nespilem.

---

4. Young, Joseph, 'An Indian's Views on Indian Affairs,' *North American Review*. Vol. CXXVIII, p. 427.

CHAPTER 6

Camas Meadows
A Race for Sitting Bull's Camp
in Canada

General Howard, with a small escort, reached General Gibbon's camp on the morning of August eleventh after the Indians had gone. Surgeons came the next day and rendered needed service to the wounded. On August thirteenth General Gibbon left three officers and fifty men to continue the pursuit with General Howard and he then took the balance of his command back to Deer Lodge, Montana.

General Howard at once took up the pursuit. Word was received that the Indians had killed eight citizens and obtained one hundred and fifty-five American horses in Horse Prairie. On August eighteenth the scouts had come upon the hostiles encamped in Camas Meadows just west of the Yellowstone National Park. The command was moved in that direction early on the morning of Sunday August nineteenth and the camp that had been occupied by the Indians was reached.

Chief Joseph had marched on, placing his women and children beyond the reach of the troops, and then returned sending his young men forward to make a night raid. The purpose was to steal the horses and mules and thus set the soldiers afoot. The raid was a success so far as the capture of the pack mules was concerned. The Indians stampeded and captured them. Chief Joseph waiting in ambush was greatly disappointed because the horses had not been captured. Later he said: "You did not picket your horses other nights, so I did not expect it this time."[1]

Three companies of cavalry under Major Sandford gave chase, recovered the mules but were ambushed, had a sharp conflict with the Indians, during which the mules were again stampeded and permanently lost. In the fight the troops lost one dead and six wounded.

The camp of the Indians was again seen not far from Henry Lake but they escaped through Tacher's Pass into Yellowstone Park. General Howard's soldiers were now in sore need of supplies so he made a quick trip to Virginia City, seventy miles away on August twenty fourth and three days later the command took up the pursuit greatly refreshed. In Yellowstone Park was found the wounded men of the Cowan party of pleasure hunters who had fallen into the hands of the Indians. One member had been killed, two wounded and Mrs. Cowan, a young lady, and her brother were carried off as prisoners. These were afterwards set at liberty by Joseph.

Major Spurgin and his pioneers helped with the wagon road repairs over rough places as they had previously done on the Lo Lo Trail.

Evidences accumulated now that the Indians no longer spared the whites. Frequent reports came to the soldiers of the murders and plunderings by the hostiles.

Colonel Miles had sent Colonel Sturgis with seven companies of the Seventh Cavalry to head off the Nez

---

1. C. E. S. Wood, 'Chief Joseph,' *Century*, vol. VI, p.140.

Percés if they should escape from the other pursuers. Chief Joseph quickly eluded this new enemy. On September tenth General Howard and Colonel Sturgis met and combined forces. Sturgis was given an addition to his force, some scouts, artillery, and cavalry and he then pushed out to overtake the Indians. He charged them gallantly and had a running fight to the Musselshell. The principal result was that he captured hundreds of ponies belonging to the Indians but the latter made good their escape.

It was now evident that the Indians were racing for Canada to join Sitting Bull.

In Clark's Valley General Howard drew up the letter to Colonel Nelson A. Miles, then located far below at Tongue River, apprising him of the situation.[2] Joseph had succeeded in getting away from his pursuers. Unless Colonel Miles should head him off he was sure of crossing the British line, thus crowning with success his most remarkable march over some of the roughest portions of the American continent.

---

2. General Howard, *Nez Percé Joseph*, p.256; compare General Miles, *Personal Recollections*, p.262.

CHAPTER 7

Battle of Bear Paw Mountain
The Surrender

Colonel Miles received the letter from General Howard on the evening of September seventeenth at his cantonment, later called Port Keogh. He instantly sent couriers in all directions to assemble available troops and ordering supplies to the upper Missouri to meet the commands of Howard and Sturgis. During the night his own troops were ferried across the Yellowstone and by early morning he was ready to hurl his command like a missile toward the fleeing Nez Percés.[1] Colonel Miles had a force of three hundred and seventy-five men, all told. This included about thirty Cheyenne Indian allies. He had a Hotchkiss gun and a twelve-pounder Napoleon. Apparently by intuition Miles marched his men across country in a direct line for the Indians who were fast approaching the Canadian line and when overtaken at Bear Paw Mountain they were only forty miles from that haven of safety.

After eluding Colonel Sturgis, Chief Joseph skirted along the Musselshell for a few miles, crossed that river, passed over the range of Snow Mountains, around Judith Mountain and across country to the Missouri which he crossed at Cow Island. Here the Indians overpowered the little garrison and destroyed a large amount of supplies, defeated another small force, mostly civilians from Port Benton and then moved, northward between the Little

---

1. G. W. Baird, 'Capture of Chief Joseph,' *International Review*, August, 1879, p. 210.

Rocky and the Bear Paw Mountains. Some of the men, escaping in a boat from Cow Island, took the news to Miles, then at the mouth of the Musselshell, fifty miles below. Miles was on familiar ground and at once moved to the point where his scouts had located the Indians. He arrived at the encampment on the morning of September thirtieth after an all night's march. The Indians were surprised. Their camp was cut in two at the first charge and most of their horses were captured. But they quickly rallied and repelled the attack so stubbornly that Miles settled down for a siege that lasted for four days. The weather had turned cold, the ground being covered with snow. The suffering of the Indians was intense.

On June twenty fifth, 1901, while visiting at Nespilem, the writer went with Chief Joseph to the blacksmith shop and while some work was being done for him the Chief talked of his last battle. With his cane he drew on the earth-floor a rough outline of the field, locating the opposed forces. The spots were indicated where had fallen his brother, Chief Ollicutt, Chief Looking Glass and Chief Too-hul-hul-sote—three chiefs lost in the last battle.

Around them lay other dead and in the camp were the suffering women and children. Chief White Bird and some of his people had escaped. Joseph could also escape and was urged to do so but in speaking of this the chief again referred to his people suffering in the camp and raising himself to his full stature he exclaimed: *"Nica waw-waw mitlite!"* which was the Chinook jargon for: *"I said I would stay here!"* at the same time pointing to his camp on the rude map.

On the evening of October fourth General Howard arrived and on the next morning he was standing at the side of Colonel Miles when Chief Joseph surrendered. He offered his rifle to Howard but at a nod from that one-armed veteran who had chased him over fourteen hundred miles the rifle was handed, instead, to Colonel Miles. It was on the occasion of his surrender that Chief Joseph made his famous speech:[2] "Tell General Howard I know his heart. What he told me before I have in my heart. I am tired of fighting. Our chiefs are killed. Looking Glass is dead. Too-hul-hul-sote is dead. The old men are all dead. It is the young men who say yes or no.. He who led on the young men is dead. It is cold and we have no blankets. The little children are freezing to death. My people, some of them, have run away to the hills, and have no blankets, no food; no one knows where they are—perhaps freezing to death. I want to have time to look for my children and see how many of them I can find. Maybe I shall find them among the dead. Hear me, my chiefs. I am tired; my heart is sick and sad. From where the sun now stands I will fight no more forever."

Thus was ended this memorable campaign. The losses in the Battle of Bear Paw Mountain to the troops were two officers and twenty-three enlisted men killed and four officers and thirty-eight men wounded. The Indians claimed a loss of thirty killed.

For the first time in Indian warfare the hostiles had refrained from torturing prisoners and from scalping or otherwise mutilating their dead enemies. The generalship that led the savages and arranged them for battle approached civilized methods to such a degree that military men have ever since expressed the greatest admiration for Chief Joseph and his skilful leadership.

---

2. Gen. G. A. Forsyth, *The Story of the Soldier*, p. 36; G. O. Shields, *Battle of the Big Hole*, p.117.

CHAPTER 8

Violation of Promises
Joseph's Band Prisoners of War

After the surrender of Joseph came the problem of what should be done with his people. There is no doubt but that, in the talks which preceded the actual surrender, Chief Joseph was promised that his people would be sent back to their homes in Idaho. C. E. S. Wood, who was General Howard's *aide-de-camp* throughout the campaign, is very emphatic on this point.[1] General Howard claims that the terms of surrender were made void when Chief Joseph allowed Chief White Bird to escape.[2] But White Bird was an older chief than Joseph and it seems hardly fair to hold Joseph responsible for that escape. At any rate General Howard gave orders to Colonel Miles to hold the Nez Percés until spring when they should be transferred to the Department of the Columbia unless higher authorities should send different instructions. Chief Joseph persistently maintained that upon his surrender he was promised that his people should be returned to Idaho.[3]

1. Wood, 'Chief Joseph,' *Century*, vol.VI, p. 142; also in a personal letter dated at Portland, Oregon, July 23, 1900.
2. Howard, 'True Story of the Wallowa Campaign,' *North American Review*, vol. CXXIX, p. 63.
3. U. S. Commissioner of Indian Affairs, *Annual Reports*, 1878, pp. XXXII-XXXV; 1881, p. 94.

Colonel Miles took the surrendered Indians to his camp on the Yellowstone where he says he intended to keep them until spring when they would be sent back to Idaho.[4] They were kept in that camp for ten days when orders came to transfer the Indians down the river to Bismarck, Dakota. From Bismarck they were ordered to be transferred to Fort Leavenworth, Kansas. Here they were kept during the winter. On December fourth the War Department reported the number of Nez Percé prisoners to be seventy-nine men, one hundred and seventy-eight women and one hundred and seventy-four children, a total of four hundred and thirty-one. When the orders came to transfer the prisoners to Indian Territory it was found that there were but four hundred and ten and of these three died *en-route* to the new quarters. Two hundred and sixty of the four hundred and seven were sick and within a few months one fourth of the whole number died.[5]

The first location in Indian Territory was about three miles from Seneca, Missouri, on the Onapaw Reservation. This proved a very unhealthy place for them and the next year they were removed to the Ponca Reservation, about fifteen miles west of the agency.

The next year, or in February 1880, a day school was opened for these Indians. It was conducted by James Reubens, an educated, Christian Nez Percé, who had journeyed from Idaho to be of some help to his people in exile. In May, 1883, Reubens closed his school and with permission of the War Department took twenty-nine Nez Percés, mostly widows and orphans of the war, back to Idaho.

---

4. Miles, *Personal Recollections*, p. 279.
5. U. S. Commissioner of Indian Affairs, *Annual Report*, 1878, pp. XXXII-XXXV.

Two years later, or in May, 1885, the rest of the Nez Percés left Indian Territory for the far north-west. Part of them went to Idaho but Chief Joseph and one hundred and twenty of his people were located on the banks of the Nespilem River, Colville Reservation in December, 1885. Agent Moore was authorized to issue them full rations.[6]

It is interesting to see what General Miles has to say about the transfer of these Indians from Indian Territory:[7]

> I frequently and persistently for seven long years urged that they be sent home to their own country, but not until 1884, when I was in command of the Department of the Columbia, did I succeed in having them returned west of the mountains to near their own country, where they have remained at peace ever since.

6. U. S. Commissioner of Indian Affairs, *Annual Report*, 1886, p. 232.
7. Miles, *Personal Recollections*, p. 280.

CHAPTER 9

Present Conditions

The week beginning with June 21, 1901, was devoted by the writer to a trip to Nespilem, on the Colville Indian Reservation, State of Washington, for the purpose of visiting Chief Joseph and his surviving warriors and to learn something of their present conditions. To get there from Spokane, Washington, one should take the Washington Central train to Wilbur and from there an all day's ride with a team crossing the Columbia River on a cable ferry.

The Colville Reservation has been cut in two. The Government has thus far neglected to pay the Indians the $1,500,000 agreed upon for the northern half. The southern half has also been thrown open for mineral entries and the familiar haunts and pasture lands of the Indians are now being overrun by a constant stream of prospectors. The writer visited one mining camp within two miles of Chief Joseph's *tepee* where the herds of Indian ponies are startled twice a day by the blasting of the rocks. At the sub-agency are two stores where these miners procure supplies.

The last census shows that there were in 1900 one hundred and twenty-seven of Chief Joseph's band at Nespilem as follows:[1]

---

1. Census manuscript at Nespilem.

Males above 18 years of age	32
Males under 18 years of age	22
Females above 14 years of age	53
Females under 14 years of age	20
Total	127

There are also on this reservation two hundred and ninety-two of Moses's band of Columbians and five hundred and seventy-five listed as Okanogans.

Chief Moses of the Columbians had been located on the Nespilem before Chief Joseph's band was brought there. He had gone to Washington City and secured many favours for his people such as a saw-mill, grist-mill, physician, blacksmith and school and a yearly salary for himself of one thousand dollars. He also procured certain allowances of agricultural implements.

Chief Joseph got no salary but the Government has issued his people regular rations of food, clothes and agricultural implements. From this fact and from the fact that he and the members of his band are supposed to ask permission if they wish to leave the reservation it is construed that Joseph's band are still practically prisoners of war.

The best agriculturalists in this vicinity are the remnants of the original Nespilems, who first occupied the land. They live in frame houses, till the soil, and with unusual pride, refuse to receive aid from the Government. If they get a reaper from the Government store-house they insist on paying for it in hay or labour.

Joseph's band, on the other hand, being supplied with everything they need, do not progress in the industrial activities. It is claimed that this idleness is a bad influence on the other Indians and the agents have been asking the Government to curtail and finally discontinue all rations to the Nez Percés.[2]

In order to get lumber for houses, barns or other purposes, the Indians go to the hills and cut the logs, which
they haul to the mill. Then they assist the Government
sawyer to cut the logs into whatever shape is desired. They
mark their own logs and keep track of all the details carrying the finished product to their homes.

The Government built for Chief Joseph a small, rough-
board, battened house and a barn on the farm he selected
about four miles from the sub-agency. The Chief will not
live in his house and the roof of his barn is broken in. He
prefers to live in the traditional *tepee*, winter and summer,
and this *tepee* he has pitched near the sub-agency so he can
be near his people and the school.

The teacher of the school, Barnett Stillwell, who has
been there for four years, says that Chief Joseph has manifested great interest in the children. He often visits the
school, at which times the Indian children would remain
almost motionless. On several occasions he administered
light punishment to some of the little ones, who were not
progressing to suit him.

Not far from the school house is the Nez Percé burial
ground. The headstones consist of poles set in the ground
with bells or feathers ornamenting the tops. It forms a
weird picture of mingled savagery and civilization. Chief
Joseph presides at every Nez Percé funeral with great and
solemn dignity.

The interior of Chief Joseph's *tepee* presents a model
appearance of neatness. Indian mats cover the floor and
in huge rolls around the edge are buffalo robes now quite
scarce among the Indians, and blankets. From one of these

---

2. U. S. Commissioner of Indian Affairs, *Annual Reports*, 1886, p. 223; 1890,
pp. 217-218; 1891, p. 442; 1892, p. 493; 1893, p. 321; 1894, p. 311; 1897, p.
290; 1898, p. 298; 1899, pp. 354-355.

rolls the chief brought a small leather trunk in which were bundles of letters he had received from white men and photographs of Indian and white friends. He knew each face and seemed glad to call up memories of his friends and relatives. At the bottom of his trunk were the eagle hat and saddle robe with which his high rank is proclaimed on all gala days.

The Indians were making great preparations for the approaching Fourth of July when they would have a celebration extending over one or two weeks. Joseph would not allow his picture to be taken until that time when his wardrobe would be in better condition for such an important operation. The Indians of this whole region show their respect for Chief Joseph by according him, without any questioning, the principal place of honour on all great festivals or celebrations.

Chief Moses had a great reputation among the Indians and whites of this section but he was dissipated. The Indians will manage at times to get liquor and Moses brought on his own death by a protracted spree. Chief Joseph never drinks intoxicants. *"Nico halo bottlum,"* as he puts it in Chinook.

Moses had two wives who survive him. Joseph is now the only Indian on the reservation who has two wives. His wives are Wa-win-te-pi-ksat, aged forty-six, and I-a-tu-ton-my, aged thirty-nine. Joseph's Nez Percé name is Hin-mah-too-Yah-lat-kekht meaning "Thunder rolling in the mountains." He claims that he is fifty-three years old but General Howard estimated his age at thirty-seven at the time of his war, which would make him sixty-one years old now.

Henry M. Steele, the sub-agent at Nespilem, says that Joseph's wives do all the work about the home and always call for the rations on issue day. He says that Joseph is appealed to when there are harnesses or other such goods to give out to the Nez Percés. The chief will designate the ones to be thus favoured but he usually begins the process by claiming one of the articles for himself.

On our visit to the *tepee*, the writer saw Joseph unharnessing his team and on another day he was saddling a pony. The sub-agent said on both occasions that it was unusual. The wives or his helpers usually did such things for him.

The Government has built for Joseph two small *ietas*, houses in which are kept his many precious properties. In one are four rifles. One of these is old and worn. Joseph says it is the one he carried through the war. Here is also seen nicely framed the certificate of Chief Joseph's appointment as an aid in the New York parade at the dedication of the Grant memorial monument on April 27, 1897. On that occasion he marched side by side with his friend Buffalo Bill.

Joseph was asked what Indian chief he considered the greatest and he answered that he thought his father, also a Chief Joseph, was the greatest. To another question he said he thought his brother Ollicutt was the next greatest chief.

Joseph has had nine children, five girls and four boys, but they are all dead. One died since living at Nespilem, two died in Indian territory and the rest died in Idaho. One daughter grew to womanhood and was married. He seems especially fond of her memory and tells what a good girl she was while showing her picture. On the back of this tintype picture is written "for Chief Joseph from his loving daughter Sarah Moses."

Bereft of his children the Chief now leads a quiet life sustained by the Government against whose authority he waged a long and bitter warfare. His last effort to regain the Wallowa Valley has been investigated by Inspector James McLaughlin who has reported strongly against the request.[3] But Joseph still longs for that old home the "Valley of Winding Waters."

In a dictated letter to the writer, dated at Nespilem, May 27, 1901, he says:

> My old home is in the Wallowa Valley and I want to go back there to live. My father and mother are buried there. If the Government would only give me a small piece of land for my people in the Wallowa Valley, with a teacher, that is all I would ask.

The white people in Wallowa Valley have named one of their towns Joseph and their newspaper was called *Chieftain* but there the sentiment ends. They enter strong protest when it is talked of sending any of the Nez Percés back to that home of their forefathers.

---

3. *Seattle Post-Intelligence*, July 8, 1900; *Chicago Record*, August 8, 1900.

LEONAUR

ALSO FROM LEONAUR
AVAILABLE IN SOFTCOVER OR HARDCOVER WITH DUST JACKET

A HISTORY OF THE FRENCH & INDIAN WAR *by Arthur G. Bradley*—The Seven Years War as it was fought in the New World has always fascinated students of military history—here is the story of that confrontation.

WASHINGTON'S EARLY CAMPAIGNS *by James Hadden*—The French Post Expedition, Great Meadows and Braddock's Defeat—including Braddock's Orderly Books.

BOUQUET & THE OHIO INDIAN WAR *by Cyrus Cort & William Smith*—Two Accounts of the Campaigns of 1763-1764: Bouquet's Campaigns by Cyrus Cort & The History of Bouquet's Expeditions by William Smith.

NARRATIVES OF THE FRENCH & INDIAN WAR: 2 *by David Holden, Samuel Jenks, Lemuel Lyon, Mary Cochrane Rogers & Henry T. Blake*—Contains The Diary of Sergeant David Holden, Captain Samuel Jenks' Journal, The Journal of Lemuel Lyon, Journal of a French Officer at the Siege of Quebec, A Battle Fought on Snowshoes & The Battle of Lake George.

NARRATIVES OF THE FRENCH & INDIAN WAR *by Brown, Eastburn, Hawks & Putnam*—Ranger Brown's Narrative, The Adventures of Robert Eastburn, The Journal of Rufus Putnam—Provincial Infantry & Orderly Book and Journal of Major John Hawks on the Ticonderoga-Crown Point Campaign.

THE 7TH (QUEEN'S OWN) HUSSARS: Volume 1—1688-1792 *by C. R. B. Barrett*—As Dragoons During the Flanders Campaign, War of the Austrian Succession and the Seven Years War.

INDIA'S FREE LANCES *by H. G. Keene*—European Mercenary Commanders in Hindustan 1770-1820.

THE BENGAL EUROPEAN REGIMENT *by P. R. Innes*—An Elite Regiment of the Honourable East India Company 1756-1858.

MUSKET & TOMAHAWK *by Francis Parkman*—A Military History of the French & Indian War, 1753-1760.

THE BLACK WATCH AT TICONDEROGA *by Frederick B. Richards*—Campaigns in the French & Indian War.

QUEEN'S RANGERS *by Frederick B. Richards*—John Simcoe and his Rangers During the Revolutionary War for America.

LEONAUR

ALSO FROM LEONAUR
AVAILABLE IN SOFTCOVER OR HARDCOVER WITH DUST JACKET

LIFE IN THE ARMY OF NORTHERN VIRGINIA *by Carlton McCarthy*—The Observations of a Confederate Artilleryman of Cutshaw's Battalion During the American Civil War 1861-1865.

HISTORY OF THE CAVALRY OF THE ARMY OF THE POTOMAC *by Charles D. Rhodes*—Including Pope's Army of Virginia and the Cavalry Operations in West Virginia During the American Civil War.

CAMP-FIRE AND COTTON-FIELD *by Thomas W. Knox*—A New York Herald Correspondent's View of the American Civil War.

SERGEANT STILLWELL *by Leander Stillwell* —The Experiences of a Union Army Soldier of the 61st Illinois Infantry During the American Civil War.

STONEWALL'S CANNONEER *by Edward A. Moore*—Experiences with the Rockbridge Artillery, Confederate Army of Northern Virginia, During the American Civil War.

THE SIXTH CORPS *by George Stevens*—The Army of the Potomac, Union Army, During the American Civil War.

THE RAILROAD RAIDERS *by William Pittenger*—An Ohio Volunteers Recollections of the Andrews Raid to Disrupt the Confederate Railroad in Georgia During the American Civil War.

CITIZEN SOLDIER *by John Beatty*—An Account of the American Civil War by a Union Infantry Officer of Ohio Volunteers Who Became a Brigadier General.

COX: PERSONAL RECOLLECTIONS OF THE CIVIL WAR--VOLUME 1 *by Jacob Dolson Cox*—West Virginia, Kanawha Valley, Gauley Bridge, Cotton Mountain, South Mountain, Antietam, the Morgan Raid & the East Tennessee Campaign.

COX: PERSONAL RECOLLECTIONS OF THE CIVIL WAR--VOLUME 2 *by Jacob Dolson Cox*—Siege of Knoxville, East Tennessee, Atlanta Campaign, the Nashville Campaign & the North Carolina Campaign.

KERSHAW'S BRIGADE VOLUME 1 *by D. Augustus Dickert*—Manassas, Seven Pines, Sharpsburg (Antietam), Fredricksburg, Chancellorsville, Gettysburg, Chickamauga, Chattanooga, Fort Sanders & Bean Station.

KERSHAW'S BRIGADE VOLUME 2 *by D. Augustus Dickert*—At the wilderness, Cold Harbour, Petersburg, The Shenandoah Valley and Cedar Creek..

www.ingramcontent.com/pod-product-compliance
Lightning Source LLC
Chambersburg PA
CBHW031855090426
42741CB00005B/507